EUDIST PRAYERBOOK SERIES:
VOLUME 6

ON THE
THRESHOLD OF ETERNITY

A SELF-DIRECTED RETREAT TO
PREPARE FOR A HAPPY DEATH

by St. John Eudes

Translated from the French
by Thomas Merton
Originally published 1946
(New York: P. J. Kenedy & Sons)

Edited by Judith Garbo
Layout by Deanna Heitschmidt

Cover image: a 40 ton marble statue of St. John Eudes in St. Peter's Basilica. Carved in 1932 by Silvio Silva, this is one of 39 large statues around the Basilica's nave and transepts honoring the founders of great religious orders.

ISBN: 978-0-9979114-7-3

Published by

EUDIST
PRESS

PO Box 3619
Vista, CA 92085-3619
eudistsusa.org

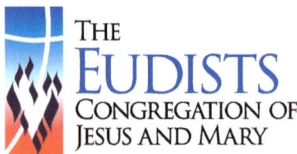

THE
EUDISTS
CONGREGATION OF
JESUS AND MARY

Table of Contents

Introduction 1

Preparation for a Happy Death.................................... 5

First Day 7
    Meditation on Submission to the Divine Will...................... 7
    Act of Acceptance 7

Second Day... 11
    Thanksgiving for All the Benefits of Your Whole Life 11

Third Day.. 13
    Confession and Satisfaction 13

Fourth Day.. 16
    Holy Communion 16

Fifth Day... 18
    Extreme Unction 18

Sixth Day.. 20
    Christ's Last Will and Testament, and the Will
       You Should Make in Its Honor.. 20
    Last Spiritual Will and Testament...................................... 25

Seventh Day 27
    The Agony and the Moment of Death 27

Eighth Day.. 29
    The Particular Judgment 29

Ninth Day 34
    Death and Burial... 34

Tenth Day.. 39
    Entrance of the Soul into Heaven and Undying Life 39

Conclusion of the Exercise 43

**Some Other Points of Advice and Necessary
Dispositions for a Holy Death** 44
    More Aspirations.. 47

Ending the Day with Jesus 51
   Act of Thanksgiving...52
   Examination of Conscience 53
   Act of Contrition Before Retiring..54
   Act of Oblation 55

Ending the Year with Jesus...57
   Prayer of Praise and Gratitude for the Close of the Year..58
   Prayer to the Blessed Virgin, at the End of the Year 60
   Annual Confession 61

Confession..62
   Preparation for Confession...62
   Thanksgiving After Confession..66
   Nature of Contrition 67
   Prayer to Beg God for Contrition 70
   Acts of Contrition 70

Holy Communion 72
   Preparation for Holy Communion 72
   Prayer Before Holy Communion 72
   Thanksgiving After Holy Communion................................. 76
   Prayer After Holy Communion..76

Preparation to Gain Indulgence 79

**Confidence and Self-Abandonment in the Hands of
God**.. 81
   Additional Points on Confidence 85

Addenda 91
   A Note on the Translator...92
   About St. John Eudes...94
   About the Eudist Family 98

Introduction

Your life will end someday. It is an indisputable truth. Most of us avoid thinking about that day. A great number of people find the concept frightening.

Your final day may seem very far away, unless you receive a diagnosis of a terminal illness. Your life may, in fact, end suddenly. Yet, in the grand scheme of things, your life is but a fleeting moment.

What happens after a person dies?

This question permeates the literature of philosophy and religion throughout all ages.

Humans hold a profound sense of *something* following our short stay on this planet. Mystics throughout time speak of interaction with something or Someone outside our physical world. Scores of reports about Near Death Experiences (NDEs) confirm this perception. In many ways, the after-life is more real — and certainly more lasting — than what one currently experiences.

Christians understand that there is indeed life beyond our feeble senses. Instead of some impersonal force or universe, we know that the unseen, eternal life relates to a Person. We understand that this Person expresses the deepest, most powerful love ever known. The name we give to this Person is God. We learn through spiritual writings, primarily the Bible, and through Church teachings that God's love is so incredible that He chose to become a man like any of us. During His earthly life, He modeled for us a life of extraordinary love — even to taking on the burden of your sins, and those of all humans, to die the most cruel death imaginable.

Unless one totally discounts an afterlife, one understands that eternity extends infinitely. Therefore, we hope to spend our eternal existence in a state of bliss. The presence of an immeasurably loving God promises an endless love of the most amazing kind. On the other hand, one might choose the opposite final destiny. If one is not at peace with God, one may reject His love and mercy. Yet, God does not cease to love the rebellious soul. Imagine spending all of eternity bathed in an immense expanse of love which the soul utterly rejects.

Are you at all prepared for the occasion? You may not have time or opportunity to prepare as your ultimate end approaches. The event might happen suddenly. Perhaps through pain, sickness, medical procedures, or mental instability you might find yourself unable to concentrate on prayer and meditation

Saint John Eudes, as the sublime pastor, wants to lead you through thinking about where you want to spend your eternity. He wants you to avoid finding yourself totally unprepared for your individual entrance into eternal life.

Through these pages, Father Eudes takes you on an expedition to explore all the facets of those final days and hours.

The saint left these instructions. Come face to face with the God of eternity. Learn of the level of perfection He exemplifies. In humility, realize your own utter failings to truly comprehend, let alone attain, His holiness and glory.

Yet, the saint does not leave you in despair. He emphasizes the profound love and mercy God holds for each of us. Father Eudes tells you straight out that God longs for your presence with Him more than we, yourself, desire it.

As proof, God Himself, lived as one of us in deep humility. He took on our sins and paid the ultimate price to atone for human failings. After all, God made each one of us as a direct result of His love for us. He made us to show forth His goodness so that we could share everlasting happiness with Him in Paradise.

Father Eudes takes you on a ten-day (or more, if you wish to spend more time to truly ponder the exercises he presents) series of meditations. He offers reflections, Biblical quotations, and prayers to direct your thoughts and will to what is needed to achieve eternal life in Paradise. Obviously, this is not easy reading. So, the saint recommends allotting some time each year for this exercise. In this way, when your time comes, you will benefit from setting the stage for your passage. These exercises will remain in your mind and heart. While they may be buried deep in your subconscious, they will bring profound comfort and quiet to your soul as you face the decisive battle of your life.

This volume presents Saint John Eudes exercises in preparation for a happy death. Father Eudes refers, in his text, to other of his writings that compliment these exercises. These include additional prayers, an evening exercise, his thoughts on ending the year with Jesus, as well as reflections on Confession and Holy Communion. He encourages us to have confidence and trust in God's great mercy. These have been inserted in the text after the ten days his concluding remarks to enhance your reflections.

The saint makes use of Scripture to enhance the prayers, and to explain his concepts. The original translators used, and sometimes paraphrased these passages according to the Douay-Rhiems Bible translation. These are left in their original form.

PREPARATION FOR A HAPPY DEATH

Death is usually preceded by such violent throes or intense weakness that the dying person is unable to direct his thoughts to God and cannot pay Him the homage owed to His divine majesty at that crucial time. Therefore, it is extremely advisable to anticipate this disability by setting aside a few days each year to carry out now what one ought rightfully to render to God at the hour of death. St. Gertrude tells us that when she had once performed this exercise, Our Lord revealed that it was most pleasing to Him, and He promised to set aside her preparation and keep it for the day of her death. You should be confident that in His goodness He will give this grace to you also, if you make use of the same exercise. For this purpose, it would be well to devote ten days to a series of ten meditations and spiritual exercises in preparation for a Christian and holy death. I now present them in due order, showing how they are to be carried out.

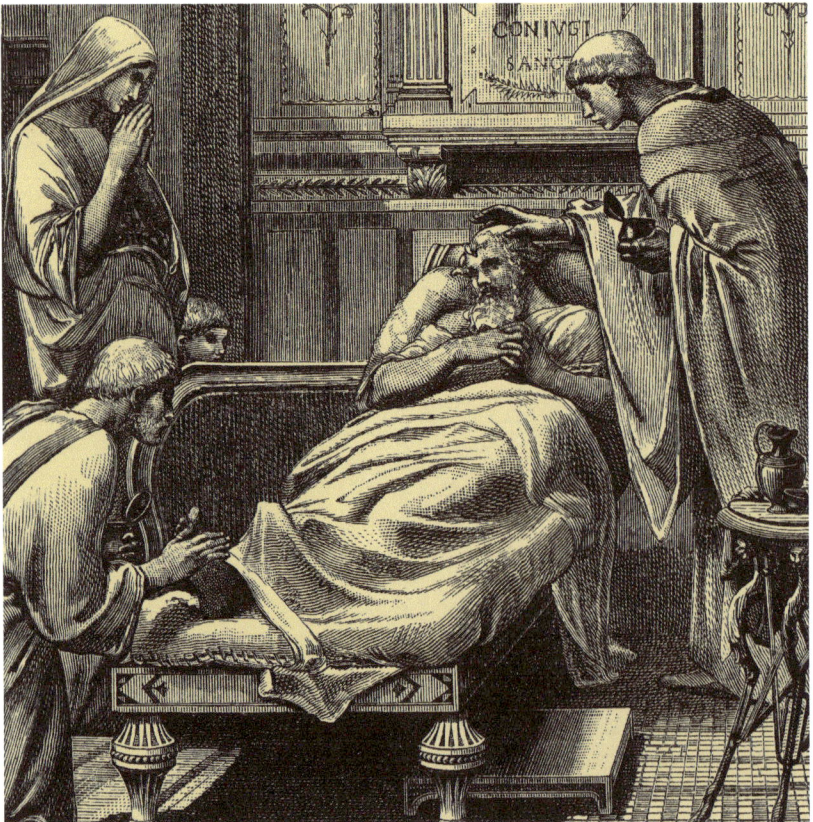

First Day

Meditation on Submission to the Divine Will

Act of Acceptance

1. O my Lord Jesus, behold me prostrate at Your feet, adoring my judge and sovereign, as You pronounce on me the sentence of death, pronounced to Adam, and in his person to all sinners, by Your words:

    "Dust you are, and into dust you shall return" (Gen. 3:19).

    In honor of Your exceeding great love and most profound humility as, prostrate upon the ground at Pilate's feet, You heard and accepted the sentence of death, spoken by the Roman governor but willed by Your Eternal Father, in honor of and in homage to His divine justice, I submit with my whole heart to the sentence of death You passed upon me even at the beginning of the world, recognizing that I have deserved it, not only by original sin, but each time I have committed sin.

2. O my God, I recognize that even if I were guilty of no sin, whether original or actual nevertheless, by Your absolute sovereignty and power over me You could in all holiness take away my life, annihilate me, and do with me as You will.

    So in honor of the very great love and in union with the deep submission with which the Blessed Virgin, Your Mother, accepted death even though she was not obliged to die, by reason of any sin, original or actual, I, too, accept death in homage to Your sovereignty, abandoning myself entirely into Your hands, that You may dispose of me in time and in eternity, according to Your holy will, for Your greater glory.

3.   O Jesus, You are eternal and immortal; You are the source
of all life, and yet You willed to die on the Cross the most
cruel and ignominious of all deaths in homage to the
justice and sovereignty, the divine and eternal life of Your
Father, and to give me a token of Your love. So, my Savior,
even if I were not obliged to die on account of my sins, and
even if (to suppose the impossible) I depended in no way
upon Your sovereignty, and even indeed if You had not
died for me in particular, I ought not only to accept death,
but even to desire to die. in order to honor Your holy death,
which is so exalted and worthy of honor that all living
creatures ought to subject themselves to death voluntarily
even if they were not already obliged to die, in homage to
the death of their Creator made Man.

Even if You had not died, O my God, all living things
ought most willingly to sacrifice their very existence to pay
homage to Your supreme and eternal being, and to bear
witness by this sacrifice that You alone are worthy to live,
and that no other being or life has any right to show itself,
but should be annihilated in Your presence as the stars of
heaven are extinguished in the light of the sun.

Your death is so worthy of honor and homage, Your life is
most worthy to be adored. With excessive love You willed
to die, not only to satisfy the justice of Your Father and to
honor His sovereignty, but also to sacrifice Your human
and temporal life for the glory of the divine and eternal
life with Your Father and Holy Spirit. By this sacrifice You
bore witness, before heaven and earth, that there is none
but the divine life alone that is worthy of existence, and
all other created life, however noble and excellent, should
be extinguished in the sight and in the presence of this
supreme and uncreated life. Therefore, in honor of Your
death, in homage to Your life, in union with the infinite
love with which you willed to die, for such great and divine
intentions, and also in honor of the burning love with
which Your Blessed Mother and all Your saints, especially
Your holy martyrs, embraced death with a very ready will
for the same intentions, I accept and embrace death with
my whole heart, in whatever form it may please You to

send it to me, that is, in the place, time, manner, and under all the circumstances it shall please You to decree.

So if You order me to die a painful or even a shameful death, or that I be left desolate and abandoned by all human help, or if I am to be deprived of the use of my senses and reason, provided You are always with me, Your holy will be done. I desire to accept and embrace all this in honor of Your most sorrowful and ignominious death, in honor of the unspeakable desolation You suffered on the Cross, abandoned even by the all-loving Father. I accept it in homage to the surrender of Your senses You made in earliest childhood. I honor You in the humiliation You suffered, being treated as a madman by Your own people, at the beginning of the preaching of the Holy Gospel, and by Herod and his court during Your Passion.

Finally, my dear Jesus, I place myself entirely in Your hands. I abandon myself so completely to Your good pleasure that I no longer desire to have any other will or desire, save to let You will, desire, and choose for me, in this and in everything else. You possess infinite wisdom and power and You have far greater knowledge, power, and will to further Your glory than I ever could have. One thing alone I beg of You, and it is that, since You died in love, by love, and for love, if I am not worthy to die for Your love or by that love, at least You may permit me to die in Your dear love.

4. O my Jesus, I implore that, just as You performed all Your actions and functions for Yourself and for all men, especially for Your children and friends, I may be permitted, in honor of and in union with Your love, to perform all these actions and render to You all due homage not only for myself but for all men, especially for all those for whom You know that I am both bound and anxious to pray with particular fervor.

O Mother of Jesus, surely it would seem that you should not have died, since you are the mother of the eternal and immortal Son of God, Who is life itself! Yet you willingly submitted to death, in homage to the most adorable death of your Son. Thus, your death is so exalted and worthy of honor that all creatures ought to subject themselves to death by their own free will, in order to honor the death of their Sovereign Lady, the Mother of their Creator. Therefore, O holy Virgin, even if I were not obliged to die, I should, nevertheless, wish to accept death freely, and offer it to you together with the death of each one who is dear to me, and of all mankind, in homage to your most holy death. I most humbly implore you, O Mother of Life, to unite my death to yours in honor of the death of your Son and to obtain from Him the grace to die in His favor and in His love.

Second Day

Thanksgiving for All the Benefits of Your Whole Life

After you have made the solemn Act of Acceptance, you should prepare for a holy death, first by thanking our Lord for all the favors you have received from Him in your whole lifetime. It is very wise to devote a day to this exercise as follows:

1. O Jesus, I contemplate and adore You as the principle and source of all good things and all temporal and eternal graces, past, present, and future, in heaven and on earth, especially those I have received from You. I refer all these graces to You, for You are their source and Your glory is their destiny. O good Jesus, who could ever describe all the favors You have done for me? They are numberless and I am utterly incapable of thanking You for them as You deserve. O dearest Lord, may all that ever was, is, or shall be in me, may all earthly and heavenly creatures, all the angels and saints, Your holy Mother, Your Holy Spirit, Your Eternal Father, all the powers of Your divinity and humanity, and all the graces and mercies which emanated from You, may all these he employed in praising You forever. May they be entirely transformed into everlasting praise of You, of all that You are together with Your Father, Yourself, and Your Holy Spirit, and of all the graces You ever imparted to Your sacred humanity, Your Blessed Mother, the angels and saints, and all creatures, and especially the graces You have given me, or would have given me if I had not stood in Your way.

    O Father of Jesus, Holy Spirit of Jesus, Mother of Jesus, angels of Jesus, saints of Jesus, and all creatures of Jesus, bless and give thanks to Him for me forever. O divine Jesus, glorify Yourself for me and return to Yourself a hundredfold all the thanks I ought to render to You.

2. O good Jesus, You know how many favors and benefits I have received from Your Blessed Mother, the angels and saints in heaven, and from many persons on earth. You know also how incapable I am of acknowledging them and giving thanks for them as I ought. So I have recourse to You, imploring You most humbly to make up for my deficiencies and to give, on my behalf, to all those souls, both in heaven and on earth, all that I ought to render to them for the benefits I have received at their hands.

3. O Mother of Grace, Mother of my God, it is through your intercession that I have received all the graces ever bestowed on me from heaven. May heaven and earth bless you for them all, on behalf of myself and of all the thoughtless persons who have received favors from you and give you no thanks whatever.

Third Day

Confession and Satisfaction

Having set aside one day to thank God for all the graces He has given you in your lifetime, it is most necessary that you devote another day to ask forgiveness for your sins and to make satisfaction to Him. To that end, you ought on this day to make a good confession, either an extraordinary confession or one marked by unusual contrition and self-abasement, with as much care and preparation as if it were to be your last confession. Acts of Contrition and other exercises for Confession will serve your purpose here also. Besides doing this, you would do well to set aside a little time during the day to meditate on this matter, in the presence of God, in the following way:

1. O most lovable Jesus, infinitely worthy of all service and love, to Whom I owe debts without number, You created me only to love and serve You. Yet I have done scarcely anything but offend You by thought, word and deed, by all my bodily senses and spiritual faculties, by my misuse of Your creatures, against all Your commandments, in countless different ways. O what sins! What ingratitude! What betrayals!

    Lord Jesus, I cast all my offenses upon Your divine love, into the abyss of Your mercies. Grant that I may be utterly changed into sorrow and contrition, with tears of blood to detest and wipe out the sins I have committed against that immense goodness, so deserving of love and honor! My God, what is there that I could ever do to make reparation for my sins? Even if I were to suffer all the torments and martyrdom in the world, I still could not of myself alone repair the insult given You by even the least of my faults.

2. O good Jesus, I offer You instead all the glory, love, and service given You by all the saints and Your most Blessed Mother, by their holy thoughts, words, and actions, by holy use of their bodily senses and their spiritual powers, by their eminent virtues and sufferings, in satisfaction for the

13

failures of my lifetime. I offer You likewise all the honor given You forever by all the angels, by the Holy Spirit, by Yourself, and by the Eternal Father, in reparation for the dishonor I have given You all my life.

3. O heavenly Father, O Holy Spirit, O angels and saints, offer up for me, to my Savior, all the love and glory you ever gave Him, in satisfaction for the wrong I have done Him by my offenses.

4. Miserable sinner that I am, by offending my God I have offended all things. I have offended the Father, the Son, the Holy Spirit, the Mother of God, all the angels and saints, and all creation, for all are concerned and offended in offense to their Creator. How, O my God, how can I make reparation for so many offenses, make satisfaction to so many persons and pay off so many debts? I know what I will do: I have my Jesus Who is in Himself an infinite wealth of virtues, merits, and good works. He has been given me to be my riches, my virtue, my sanctification, my redemption and reparation. I shall offer Him to the Eternal Father, to the Holy Spirit, to the Blessed Virgin, to all the angels and all the saints in reparation and satisfaction for all the faults I have committed. O holy Father, O divine Spirit, I offer all the love and honor that my Jesus gave you by all His divine thoughts, words, and actions, by His divine employment of all the members of His body and of His soul, by all His glorious virtues and heroic sufferings, in satisfaction for all the offenses I have committed against You all my life long.

O holy Virgin, O holy angels, O blessed saints, I offer you my treasure and my all, my Savior Jesus Christ. I conjure [call forth or summon] you to draw upon His infinite storehouse of merit whatever you require in payment and satisfaction for all the debts I owe you, by reason of my sins and negligences.

5. O my Jesus, my divine Redeemer, make reparation for all my faults, and by Your very great mercy atone for all my sins committed against the Eternal Father, Yourself, the Son, the Holy Spirit, Your most Blessed Mother, the angels and saints, and all persons I have offended. I give myself to You to do and suffer in atonement whatsoever may be pleasing to Your holy will, accepting now all the sufferings of body or spirit that I may have to bear, whether in this world or in the next, in satisfaction for my sins.

6. O most holy Virgin, I have so many obligations to serve and venerate you; yet I have so little honored and so greatly offended you by offending your Son! I beg your forgiveness, O Mother of Mercy, and I offer You in satisfaction all the honor ever accorded you in heaven and on earth. I implore all the angels and saints, the Holy Spirit, your Son, and the Eternal Father to supply for my deficiencies, and fill up the measure of glory I ought to have rendered to you all my life long.

Fourth Day

Holy Communion

Holy Communion is the most precious and effective means given you by God to render to Him all the honor and service you owe to Him. To prepare for a holy death, you should make a point of taking one day of this exercise to dispose yourself for an exceptionally well-prepared Communion, marked by extraordinary devotion and approached with as much care and recollection as if it were to be your last. The exercise I drew up for Holy Communion will prove sufficient for this purpose, provided you use it profitably.

Let me merely tell you that you should offer this special Communion to our Lord:

1. in honor of all that He is in Himself and towards you;

2. in thanksgiving for all the effects of His love for His Father and for all creatures, but especially for you;

3. in satisfaction for all the dishonor and pain given him by all the sins of the world, especially by your own;

and

4. for the fulfilment of the plans of His divine providence for all men, especially for you.

Offer yourself to the Eternal Father, begging Him to unite you with the surpassing love of His paternal heart when He received His Son, Jesus Christ, into His bosom on the day of the Ascension. Give yourself to Jesus and beg Him to unite you with the most ardent love and profound humility with which He instituted the holy Sacrament of the altar, on the eve of His death. Offer yourself to the Blessed Virgin, to St. John the Evangelist, to St. Mary Magdalen, and St. Mary of Egypt, and all the other saints, praying that they may cause you to participate in the love and fervor, the humility, purity and sanctity with which they received holy Viaticum.

After you have received Communion and made the usual thanksgiving to our Lord with unusual fervor, adore His divine plans from all eternity for you. Beg Him to forgive all the obstructions you have ever placed in the way of their operation. Fervently beg Him not to let you die until He has completed the plans of His goodness and the work of His grace in your soul. Give yourself to Him with a great desire and mighty resolution to work manfully to consummate His work in you, and to destroy in yourself everything that might stand in His way, so that you may be able to repeat to Him, on the last day of your life, His words to the heavenly Father on Good Friday:

"I have finished the work which You gave Me to do" (John 17:4).

Fifth Day

Extreme Unction

You do not know whether you will be able to concentrate on God when you receive the sacrament of Extreme Unction, (assuming that it may please Him to grant this grace). It would, therefore, be a good thing to devote the fifth day to acquit yourself of the obligations to our Lord to this holy sacrament and to prepare for a meritorious reception of Extreme Unction.

1. O Jesus, I adore You as the author of the holy sacrament of Extreme Unction, and as the source of its priceless graces, which You have acquired and merited for us by the shedding of Your precious blood.

    I refer to You all the graces You ever produced in souls through Extreme Unction. I bless You a thousand times for all the glory You have given to Yourself by this last sacrament. I adore the infinite design of Your providence in the institution of Extreme Unction and I surrender myself to the accomplishment of Your divine plan for me according to Your holy will. I implore You most humbly to grant me the grace of receiving this sacrament at the end of my life. If I should not be able to receive it, I implore You to produce in my soul, by Your great mercy, the same graces I would acquire by its reception.

2. O Jesus, I adore You in the holy anointing of Your sacred body in the last days of Your life by St. Mary Magdalen, and at Your burial by St. Nicodemus and St. Joseph of Arimathea. I offer You all the holy unctions ever performed, in this last sacrament, upon the bodies of all Christians who have received it or ever shall do so, in honor of and in homage to the divine anointing of Your deified body.

3. O good Jesus, I adore You as High Priest to Whom, before all others, belongs the right of conferring all the sacraments. I give myself to You as High Priest and implore You to inspire in my soul all the dispositions required for the fruitful reception of Extreme Unction and to produce in

me all the graces represented by its consoling ceremonies. In order to dispose myself for its reception, O my Savior, behold I cast myself down at Your feet, accusing myself before You and Your heavenly court of all my sins, most humbly begging Your forgiveness with all the humility and contrition I can muster, with my whole heart imploring You, together with Your Blessed Mother and all the angels and saints, to ask forgiveness from Your Eternal Father, and to offer to Him in satisfaction for my sins the full measure of Your infinite merits and sufferings.

O good Jesus, come into my soul and into my heart. Come to bring me Your holy peace and to destroy in me all that might disturb the peace and repose of my spirit. Come unto me, and with Your precious blood purify me of the foulness of my sins. Come to grant me full and total absolution, indulgence and remission of all my sins.

O most kind Jesus, I offer You all the senses and members of my body and all the powers of my soul. Anoint me, I beg You, with the sacred oil that ever flows from Your divine heart, that is, with the oil of Your grace and mercy and, by this heavenly anointing, cleanse me of the evil effects of my sins. O dearest Jesus, I offer You the holy employment of bodily senses and spiritual powers ever made by Your divine self, by Your Blessed Mother, and all the saints, in satisfaction for my abuse or misuse of the members and senses of my body and the faculties of my soul. May it please You to grant me the grace to employ them in future only for Your pure glory.

Finally, O most amiable Jesus, may it please You to give me Your holy blessing. Ask the beneficent Father and the Holy Spirit to bless me with You, so that this divine and mighty benediction may destroy in me all that displeases You, and transform me utterly into eternal benediction and praise of the Father, the Son, and the Holy Spirit.

Sixth Day

Christ's Last Will and Testament, and the Will You Should Make in Its Honor

On this day you should prepare to make a will, in imitation and honor of the final testament of Jesus Christ on earth. In the presence of God, you should meditate on the infinitely adorable legacy left by Christ and consider how to make your own will in the same spirit with similar dispositions. This may be done in the following manner:

> O Jesus, I adore You in the last days of Your life. I adore every aspect and event of these last days, but especially Your divine testament pronounced in the Cenacle, on Mount Olivet, and from the Cross. I adore, bless and glorify the supreme love for Your Father, the most burning charity towards us and all the other holy dispositions of Your last testament to mankind.

> In Your last will there are five bequests:

> The first bequest is to Your enemies, for,

> O Wonder of wonders, O immensity of goodness, Your first word and first prayer on the Cross is for Your enemies, begging the Father to pardon them, in the very hour when they were crucifying You.

> The second bequest is to the Heavenly Father, the final gift of Your holy soul with these words:

>> *"Father, into Your Hands I commend My Spirit"* (Luke 23:46).

> These words were uttered not only with reference to Your deified soul, but to my soul and to the souls of all who belong to You, which were all at that moment before Your sight, and You looked upon them as Your own possession, forming all together but one soul with Yours, by virtue of their most intimate union. When You said to the Father:

>> *"Father, into Your hands, I commend My Spirit."*

You spoke for Yourself and for me; You commended my soul together with Yours into the hands of Your Father, addressing this prayer to Him Who is at once Your Father and mine, in Your name and my own, against the hour when my soul shall leave my body. You made the offering of my soul with the same love with which You said Father in general, not my Father in particular, to show that You regarded Him not only as Your own special Father, but as the common and universal Father of all Your brethren and members. You prayed to Him not only for Yourself in particular, but also in general for all who belong to You, with filial confidence and love, as much for Yourself as for them, for which may You be loved and blessed forever.

The third bequest in Your Will concerns the Blessed Mother, to whom You gave that which was most dear to You after herself, the beloved disciple, St. John the Evangelist. At the same time there were represented in the person of St. John all the other disciples and children, until the end of time. When You said to Mary the words,

> *"Woman, behold your Son"* (John 19:26),

You gave her not only St. John, but all other Christians to be her children. Reciprocally, in saying to St. John the words:

> *"Behold your Mother."* (John 19:27),

You gave to him and also to all Christians, represented in his person, Your most precious possession in the order of created beings, namely, Your most Blessed Mother. You gave her to them to be their mother just as she was Your Mother, imparting to them Your precious relationship and character with her. That was the reason You called her no longer Your mother, but *"Woman"* to show the transfer to us of Your relationship to her as Son, and the gift to us, as mother, of her who was about to cease to be Your mother for a time by reason of her Son's death. So, good Jesus, You bequeathed me in Your will to Your Blessed Mother, not only as a servant and subject, but actually as a son. You gave her to me not only as my queen and lady, but in the most honorable and lovable character there is — that of a mother. O love! O excess of goodness! May the whole world be transformed into love for so great a goodness!

The fourth bequest in Your will is particularly ours and concerns us so diversely that it seems to have been made for us alone.

1. During Your last days on earth, O Jesus, You expressed a surpassing and extraordinary love, assuring us that

    Your Father loves us as He loves You (John 17:23),

    and that

    You love us as Your Father loves You (John 15:9).

    You consequently urge us to

    love one another as You have loved us (John 13:34).

2. You likewise commended us with most particular affection to the most exalted and powerful persons most dear to You, by whom You are most loved in heaven and on earth — that is, Your Eternal Father and Your divine Mother. To the Father just before setting out on the road to Calvary, You addressed a beautiful prayer:

    "Holy Father, keep them in your name whom You have given Me. Not for them only do I pray but for them who through their word shall believe in Me" (John 17:11-20).

22

While hanging on the Cross, You placed our souls in His hands together with Your own, as has been said. You also commended us to Your divine Mother.

3. We share in Your will because in Your last, solemn and public prayer, You obtained from the heavenly Father the greatest favors that could have been asked of Him, or that He could have given us. Here are the prayers You addressed to Him for us:

> *"Father, I will that where I am, they also whom You have given Me may be with Me"* (John 17:24),

that is,

> that they should have their dwelling and take their rest with Me forever in Your bosom and Your Fatherly heart.

> *"Just Father, may the love wherewith You have loved Me, be in them"* (John 17:25-26),

that is to say:

> Love them as You love Me, love them with the greatest, the most burning and most divine love that could ever possibly exist. Look upon them as You regard Me; love them with the very heart with which You love Me; treat them as You treat Me; give them all that You give Me.

> *"That they may be one, as You, Father, in Me and I in You; that they also may be one in Us...I in them, and You in Me: that they may be made perfect in one"* (John 17:21-23).

O dearest Lord, what love! What more could You ask the Father for us?

4. We share in Your will because You gave us the most rare and precious gift, Your Eternal Father to be our Father, praying Him to love us as He loves You, as His children with sublime paternal love. You gave us Your Blessed Mother to be our mother. You gave us Your most holy body in the Eucharist, Your holy soul on the Cross in death with the words:

"I lay down my life for my sheep" (John 10:15).

You gave Your precious blood to the very last drop, Your life, merits, sufferings, humanity, and divinity, as expressed in these words:

"The glory which You have given Me, I have given to them" (John 17:22).

You gave up all without reserve. O dearest Lord, how admirable is Your goodness, poured forth for us in the very hour when we were causing You to suffer so many evils! How can we love You so little and think so seldom of You? How can so great a love be held so cheap and be so despised by those whom You love so much?

The fifth and last bequest in Your will was made on Mount Olivet when, departing from the apostles and ascending into heaven, You gave them Your holy blessing. We share in this bequest also, for in imparting Your blessing to the holy apostles and disciples You blessed all of us, each one in particular, for we were all just as much present in Your sight then as we are now. May heaven and earth bless You, O Author of all gifts, and may all things in heaven and earth be transformed into eternal blessings from You.

Such, good Jesus, are the five clauses of Your admirable will, in honor of which I desire. if it please You, to draw up my own testament as follows:

Last Spiritual Will and Testament

1. O most kind Jesus, in honor of and in union with the
    love with which You shed Your blood and died for Your
    enemies and prayed to Your Father to pardon those
    who crucified You, with my whole heart I fully forgive
    all those who have ever offended or injured me, and I
    implore You to grant them full pardon. I offer myself
    to You to do and suffer whatever may please You for
    their sake, even to shed my blood and die for them, if
    necessary. So, too, in all the humility I can muster, I
    beg all whom I have ever offended or displeased in my
    whole life to forgive me, and I give myself to You to
    make whatever satisfaction to them You may desire.

2. In honor of and in union with the exceeding great
    love, the most perfect confidence and all the other
    dispositions with which You commended Your soul
    and all the souls that belong to You into the hands of
    Your Father, I surrender my soul, with the souls of all
    those for whom I am bound to have special concern,
    into the gentle hands and the most loving heart of
    the divine Father, Who is my God, my Creator and
    my most lovable Father, that He may dispose of them
    according to His good pleasure. I trust that His infinite
    goodness will place them with Your soul, good Jesus,
    in His Fatherly bosom, there to love and bless Him
    eternally with You, according to the desire of Your soul,
    expressed in the words:

    > *"Father, I will that where I am, they also whom You have
    > given Me may be with Me"* (John 17:24).

3. In honor of and in union with Your great charity in
    giving all Your friends and children to Your most
    Blessed Mother, I resign into her hands all those
    entrusted to my care, imploring You, good Jesus, to
    commend them Yourself to Your Virgin Mother. I
    implore her with my *whole heart, by* Your very great love
    for her and hers for You, and by the same love with
    which You gave her Your friends and children, to look

upon them henceforth as her children in a more special way, and to be their Mother.

4. In honor of and in union with the exceedingly powerful love whereby You commended me to Your Father on Your last day, and begged Him, on my behalf, for such great favors, giving me all that was most dear to You, with such extraordinary tokens of that love, urging me also to love my neighbor as You loved me: I commend to You all those whom You know I should commend particularly to You, and beg You on their behalf for all that You asked for me from Your Eternal Father on Good Friday. I abandon myself to You to love You as You love the Father and as the Father loves You. I give myself also to You to love my neighbor as You loved me, and to shed my blood and give my life for him, if it is Your holy will.

5. O Jesus, God of all blessings, I adore You in the last moment of Your sojourn on earth, upon Mount Olivet, as You left the earth to ascend into heaven. I adore You giving Your most holy blessing to Your Blessed Mother, Your apostles and disciples; I adore the exceeding great love and all the other dispositions which filled Your divine soul when You imparted this supreme blessing as is related in the Holy Gospel (Luke 24:50).

    O good Jesus, behold me prostrate at Your feet, in union with the humility and the other holy dispositions of the Blessed Mother and the holy apostles and disciples as they received Your blessing. I most humbly implore You, by all Your love for them, and theirs for You, to give now to me and to all I have commended to You, Your most holy blessing, so that by the power of that divine blessing all that displeases You in me may be destroyed and may be altogether transformed into everlasting praise, love, and benediction of You.

Seventh Day

The Agony and the Moment of Death

You shall consider this day as if it were to be your last. You must strive to spend it with as much care and devotion as if you had only this one day in which to love God. For this purpose, you should apply yourself to the contemplation and adoration of our Lord in the last day of His life on earth, and to do everything in union with the holy and divine dispositions of His last actions. With the last day of your life in view, you should implore Jesus to unite you to His dispositions and foster them in your heart, that you may be of the number of those of whom it is said:

"Blessed are the dead who die in the Lord" (Rev.14:13),

that is, who die in the dispositions of the death of our Lord Jesus Christ. Similarly, you should consider and honor the Blessed Virgin on the last day of her life, uniting yourself to her dispositions, offering her the last day of your life. The prayers addressed to Jesus Christ and His Blessed Mother for the end of the year should also serve your purpose here. I may also add at this point that it is a good thing on this day to adore Jesus and honor His most holy Mother in their agony and death, offering your agony and death in union with theirs, imploring them to bless and sanctify your death by their own. It is also most beneficial to adore the infinite power of the divine love that caused the death of Jesus and of His most holy Mother, for they both died of love and by love.

You should implore that divine love to cause you to die with Jesus and His divine Mother, and to consume and sacrifice your life in its sacred flames. You should also honor the holy martyrs and all saints in their agony and death; offer them your agony and death, in union with their own, begging them to unite you with their holy dispositions as they prepared for death. Implore them specially to associate you with all the love and glory they gave to Our Lord on the last day of their life and at the moment they died for Him. You should pray especially to St. John the Evangelist, St. Mary Magdalen and

27

the good thief who died with Jesus, and all the other saints who were present at the death of the Son of God, that through the merits of their privilege in being near Him in death, they may give you special assistance at the hour of your own death.

On this same day it would be most advisable to read the Passion of Our Lord, the seventeenth chapter of St. John, containing His last words and prayers before setting forth to be crucified, as well as the prayers of Holy Mother Church for the agonizing soul, which are to be found at the end of the Breviary. For you do not know whether you will be in a fit state on the last day of your life to complete these preparations for a holy death. Hence, it is a good thing to anticipate that day, and to read the Passion of Our Lord and the above-mentioned prayers with all the devotion you would wish to put into them at the hour of death, and all the devotion with which they have ever been read by the whole Church. Above all, when you read the seventeenth chapter of St. John, which contains the last words and prayers of Jesus, give yourself to Him in a sincere effort to pronounce these words and prayers in union with His love, dispositions, and intentions when He spoke them, imploring Him to foster in your heart these sublime dispositions in preparation for the last day of your life and to produce the effects of these holy words.

Finally, cast yourself down at the feet of Jesus and His most holy Mother, to implore them to give you their most holy blessing.

O Jesus, O Mother of Jesus, give me your holy blessing for the last moment of my life. By your great goodness, grant that the last moment of my life may be consecrated to the glory of the last moment of yours, and that my last breath may be an act of most pure love for you!

Eighth Day

The Particular Judgment

It is a most holy practice, when present at a deathbed, to kneel down at the moment the person dies, to adore the advent of the Son of God, who comes to judge that soul right there in the body, where it remains until it is consigned elsewhere by His judgment. It would be quite easy to prove that the Son of God thus comes to judge the soul at the hour of death, because several passages of Holy Scripture clearly speak of it. This is not, however, the place to do so. All I have to say for the present is that if it is beneficial to adore the Son of God in the exercise of His judgment upon others at the hour of death, how much more should you adore Him in His coming for you and His judgment at the hour of your death. Therefore, you must render to Him now, freely and out of love, the honor that shall be obligatory when your end comes. Hence, this day shall be spent in this exercise, performed as follows:

1. O Jesus, You are the Saint of saints and sanctity Itself, infinitely above all sin and imperfection. Yet, I behold You prostrate with Your face to the earth at the feet of the all-just Father in the Garden of Olives, and the following day at the feet of Pilate, where the Eternal Father contemplates You as the victim who has taken upon Himself all the sins of the world, giving Himself without reserve for the ransom of mankind. You have taken the place of all sinners and borne the heavy judgment of our sins by dying on the Cross for our salvation. You accept that judgment with most perfect submission, most profound humility and most ardent love for Your Father and for us. O Jesus, I adore and glorify You in this judgment and in all the holy dispositions of humiliation, contrition, submission, and love with which You suffered to be judged and condemned to save us.

2. In honor of and in union with these dispositions, behold me prostrate at Your feet, great Jesus, adoring You as my sovereign judge. I most willingly submit myself to Your supreme power. I infinitely rejoice that You have sovereign power over me and over all men and angels. A thousand times I bless the Eternal Father for having given You this power. I affirm sincerely that if, to imagine the impossible, You did not have this power, and I did have it, I would want to strip myself of it to give it to You; if I were not subject to Your power to judge me, I should wish to subject myself voluntarily to that power, out of homage to Your divine justice and to the condemnation You underent from Your Father during Your holy Passion.

3. O Jesus, I adore You in Your coming at the hour of my death and at the moment of Your judgment of my soul. I adore now every aspect and detail of my particular judgment. May it please You to grant me now some measure of the divine light by which You will clearly show me every event of my whole life, compelling me to give an account of everything. Grant me a share in the zeal for justice with which You will be avenged for my offenses, so that I may from now on see my sins clearly and make reparation by perfect contrition, horror and detestation for these same sins.

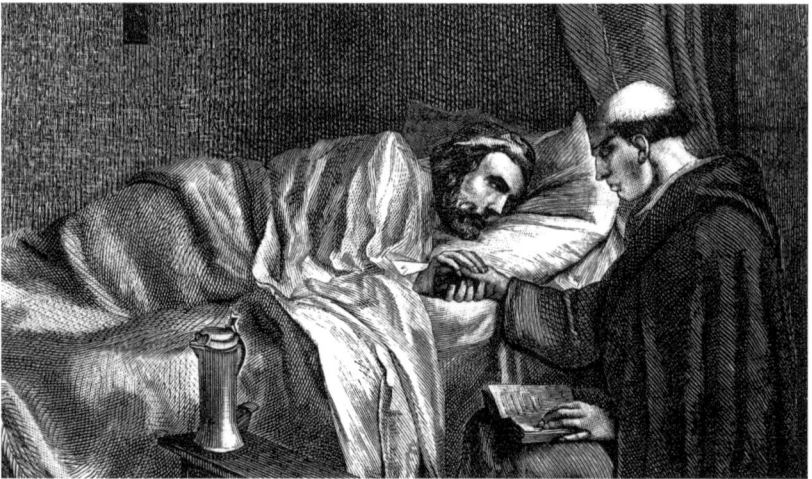

4. O my God, how many sins I have committed against You all my life, by thought, word and deed, in every way! They can not be numbered, I confess; and I accuse myself before You, Your Blessed Mother, before all the angels and saints, and, if it be Your holy will, before the whole world. I accuse myself of my sins just as they are in Your sight, as You know them. If only I could see my offenses as You see them!

If only I knew myself as You know me, and as I shall see and know myself in Your light at the moment of judgment! How I shall be confounded and humiliated then by the realization of what I am! What horror my crimes will awaken in me! What regret, what anguish at having so little loved and so greatly offended so transcendent a goodness as Yours! How quickly will I then accuse and condemn my own self! Indeed there will be no need of any other judge, for I shall be the first to pass sentence upon my own misdeeds and ignominy.

5. But why wait until that final hour? Lord, at this very moment I surrender myself to the zeal of Your divine justice and to the spirit of your just hatred and righteous horror for sin. In honor of and in union with Your extreme hatred of sin, I hate and detest all my sins; I hold them in abhorrence; I renounce them forever; I offer myself to You to suffer for them all the penance You shall order. Casting myself down before Your face, in the ultimate depths of abjection, to which, O great God, I have deserved to be reduced by my sins, I pronounce against myself, in the presence of heaven and earth, that final sentence. Since I, who am nothing but a worm of the earth, a handful of ashes and mere nothingness, have in so many ways offended so exalted and great a majesty, there are no tortures, either on earth, in Purgatory, or in hell, capable of worthily expiating my sin, without the intervention of Your mercy and the power of Your precious blood. For all these torments are finite, while the offense of my sins is infinite, since they offend an infinite majesty, and consequently deserve an infinite punishment.

So, my sovereign Judge, falling down once more at Your feet, and in the nethermost depths of the bottomless pit of my sins, I adore and bless and love You with my whole heart, as pronouncing the sentence that You shall pronounce at the hour of my death, and I voluntarily, with all the love possible to me, submit to this sentence, whatever it may be, telling You with the royal prophet, with all the power of my will:

"You are just, O Lord, and Your judgment is right" (Ps. 119:137).

I most obediently accept anything it may please You to ordain in my regard, in time and eternity, giving myself to You to bear not only all the sufferings of Purgatory, in homage to Your divine justice, but any other penalty You may impose upon me. I take no thought of what is to become of me nor of what is to be done to me in time and eternity, provided only that the wrong and dishonor I have done You may be made good, no matter what the cost.

Yet, O God of mercy, do not permit that I should be numbered among those who will never love You. O most merciful Lord, what am I that You condescend to open Your blessed eyes to look upon me, to summon me into Your presence in judgment and to exercise Your justice upon me? It is all too true that I deserve Your mercy far less than Your justice. But, O Savior of my soul, remember that You willed to be judged for me, and that You are most worthy that my sins should be forgiven in You, since You asked the all merciful Father to pardon them for me. Yet, Lord, enter not into judgment with Your miserable and unworthy servant, but offer for me to Your Father the judgment You sustained for my sins, and pray that His divine forgiveness be granted, not to me but to You.

O Father of mercy, I confess that I have deserved to bear the stern weight of Your judgments, and that I am not worthy that You should give me the least grace, nor that You should pardon the very smallest of my sins. I offer You the terrible judgment Your Son sustained for my faults, and I implore You to pardon them, not to me, but to Your beloved Son, who begs Your forgiveness on my behalf, and to give Him, also, all the graces I need for Your service. All possible punishments in the world, visited upon me, are incapable of giving You fitting satisfaction for the very least of my crimes. Your Son alone can make perfect reparation for the dishonor I have given You. So I offer to You, and I implore Him to offer with me, all that He did and suffered in His whole life, and all the honor He ever rendered to You, whether by Himself or through His Blessed Mother, His angels, and all His saints.

O Mother of Mercy, Mother of Jesus, O angels and saints of Jesus, offer to God all your merits and works on my behalf and all the glory you ever gave Him, in satisfaction for my offenses and implore Him to treat me not according to the rigor of His justice, but the multitude of His mercies, in order that I may love and bless Him with you forever.

Ninth Day

Death and Burial

Since Jesus Christ, our Lord, willed to pass through all the phases of human life, in order to honor His Eternal Father and to bless and sanctify them for you, you should also have a holy zeal for honoring Him particularly in each of the phases of His life, and to consecrate all the states, in which you have been and are to be, to the honor of each aspect of His mortal life. Following this teaching, after you have adored Him in the last moment of His life, dedicating to Him your own last moment, it is now very appropriate to adore Him in the state of death, in which He remained for three days, and to consecrate to Him the condition of death in which you are to be from the last moment of your life until the day of the general resurrection, as follows:

1. O Jesus, You are eternal life and the source of all life, yet I behold You cold in the darkness and shadow of death. I see You bid farewell, for a little while, to Your most lovable Mother, to Your dearly beloved apostles and disciples, and to all Your friends left bathed in tears, in the greatest mourning and lamentation of all time. I contemplate Your holy soul separated from Your divine Body, with which it had so holy, so close, and so sublime a union. I see this same body, more holy and sacred than all the heavenly bodies (I mean than all those in all the heavens, and more than the empyrean [celestial sphere of] heaven itself), lying in a sepulchre, among the rocks in the dust. O my Jesus, I adore, praise and glorify You thus. I offer You all the honor rendered to You in this state by Your holy Mother, by St. Mary Magdalen, by the holy apostles and disciples, by the angels, by the holy souls You freed from Limbo and by the whole Church, with all the glory Your Father gave You, and which You now enjoy in heaven, in recompense for that humiliation You did bear on earth. I offer You the state of death which will one day be mine, in honor of that state of

death in which You remained before the resurrection. I offer You the separation from the company of my friends and relatives that I shall one day have to bear, in honor of the most bitter separation which You suffered, torn from the most sweet company of Your dearest Mother, of Your dearly beloved apostles and disciples. I offer You all the sorrow and the tears of my relatives and friends in honor of the sorrow and tears of Your harrowed Mother and sorrowing apostles. I offer You the separation of my soul from Your sacred Body. I offer You all the states of my soul, until its reunion with its body, whatever they may be, in homage to the state in which Your holy soul existed during the time it was separated from Your body. I offer You the burial of my body and all the actions that shall be done in performing this burial, in honor of the burial of Your holy body. In honor of and in union with the same love with which You, O good Jesus, willed that Your sacred body should lie upon the dust within a hollow rock, and by which You have so often given me this same body in Holy Communion, although I am nothing but a worm of the earth, I most willingly surrender my body to the ground and to the worms. I consent to be reduced to ashes and dust, but only on condition, O crucified Savior, that all the grains of dust into which my flesh and bones shall crumble, may be so many voices praising and glorifying without interruption the adorable mystery of Your burial, and that I may thus sing with the holy psalmist:

"All my bones shall say: Lord, who is like to You?" (Ps. 35:10).

2. O divine Jesus, even though Your body and soul were separated, nevertheless they are continually united to Your divinity. Thus, they never ceased to be worthy of infinite honor and adoration. Therefore, I adore Your holy soul in its descent into Limbo. I adore all that happened in Your soul and all the efforts produced in the souls of the holy patriarchs in Limbo. I also adore Your body in the tomb, in all Its members, for there is no part of It that is not infinitely adorable. I adore you, O most holy eyes of my Savior's body. I adore you, O sacred ears of my God. I adore and praise you, O most blessed mouth and tongue of Him Who is the word and eternal utterance of the Father. I adore and bless you, O most divine hands and feet of my Lord. I adore and love you, O most amiable heart of Jesus. Alas, my Beloved, Your perfect body is lifeless because of my sins! Those sacred eyes, that by their sweet aspect gave joy to all who came in contact with You, are now darkened by the shadow of death. Those holy ears, always open to hear the cries and prayers of all unhappy creatures, are now closed and hear no more. Those divine lips, which pronounced the words of life, have become mute and speak no words. Those blessed hands that wrought so many miracles are lifeless and still. Those holy feet, so often wearied for the salvation of the world, are no longer able to walk. Above all, the most loving heart of my Jesus, the most exalted and noble throne of divine love, is without life or feeling. Ah, my dear Jesus, who has brought You to this pitiable state? My sins and Your love! Cursed and detestable sin, how I abhor you! O love of my Savior, may I love You, may I bless You without ceasing!

3. O good Jesus, I surrender myself completely to the power of Your holy love. I implore You by that love, to reduce me now into a state of death that may imitate and honor Your state of death. Utterly extinguish in me the life of sin and of the old Adam. Cause me to die to the world, to myself and to all that is not You. Mortify my eyes, ears, tongue, hands, feet, heart, and

all the other powers of my body and soul, so that I may no longer be able to see, nor hear, speak, taste, act, walk, love, think, will, nor make any other use of all the parts of my body or the faculties of my soul, save in accordance with Your good pleasure, led by the guidance of Your divine Spirit.

4. O my well-beloved Jesus, I give myself to You to derive the benefits of these words of Your Apostle:

    "You are dead: and your life is hid with Christ in God" (Col. 3:3).

    Hide me utterly with You in God. Bury my mind, my heart, my will and my being, so that I may no longer have any thoughts, desires, or affections, any sentiments and dispositions other than Your own. Just as the earth changes and transforms into itself the bodies buried within it, may You change and transform me completely into Yourself. Bury my pride in Your humility, my coldness and tepidity in the fervor of Your divine love, and all my other vices and imperfections into Your holy virtues and perfections so that, just as the earth consumes all the corruption of the body buried in it, so all the corruption of my soul may be consumed and annihilated in Your divine perfections.

5. O Mother of Jesus, I honor and revere you in the state of your death and burial. I offer you all the honor then given you by the angels and holy apostles. I thank you for all the glory you gave to the death and burial of your Son by your own. I offer you my own death and burial, imploring you to obtain for me, by your holy prayers, the grace that every aspect of my earthly end may pay everlasting homage to the death and burial of your spotless self and of your beloved Son, our Savior.

Tenth Day

Entrance of the Soul into Heaven and Undying Life

Even though we are most unworthy to see the face of God and to be admitted into the blessed company of the citizens of heaven, it is, nevertheless, most certain that the Father, the Son, the Spirit, the Blessed Virgin, all the angels, and all the saints eagerly desire to behold you soon joined with them, to be overwhelmed as they are in torrents of the heavenly and unspeakable delights of divine love which reigns with fulness in heaven. We ought to have great trust that, in the goodness of God, this will one day he realized for us. Our greatest consolation in this world ought to be the thought and expectation of that day when we shall begin to love and glorify God in all perfection. What rejoicings we should voice with the royal prophet, at the vision and thought of that blessed day:

> *"I rejoiced at the things that were said to me: We shall go into the house of the Lord"* (Ps. 122:1).

> *"Blessed are they who dwell in Your house, O Lord: they shall praise You forever and ever."* (Ps. 83:4).

Surely if you celebrate the day of your birth into the life of grace by holy Baptism, how much more should you celebrate the feast of your entrance into heaven and your birth into the life of glory! Anticipate that day, and begin now to celebrate that feast by means of the following exercises:

1. O Jesus, I adore, praise and glorify You countless times at the moment of Your triumphant entrance into heaven. I offer You all the glory, love and praises that were given to You in welcome by the Father, the Holy Spirit, Your Blessed Mother, and all the angels. I also honor Your Blessed Mother in the moment of her assumption into Paradise. I offer her all the glory and praises that were given her by the omnipotent Father, by her beloved Son, Yourself, Your Holy Spirit, all the angels and all the saints. I offer to You and to Your glorious Mother, my own entrance into Paradise, which,

I hope, by Your great mercy, to make one day, in honor of the glorious and triumphant entry of Your Ascension and her Assumption. O my most adorable Jesus, I desire to consecrate everything that ever was, is and shall be in me, in time and in eternity, to the honor and homage of You and Your most holy Mother.

2. O most admirable and most adorable Trinity, I adore, bless and magnify You infinitely for all that You are in Your manifold works of mercy and justice toward me and to all Your creatures, in heaven, on earth and in hell. I offer You all the adoration, love, glory, praise and benediction accorded You forever. O my God, how I rejoice to behold You so full of greatness, of marvels, of glory, and joy! It is enough. I desire no other glory, felicity, or happiness, in eternity save to behold the incomprehensible glory, felicity, and happiness of Him Whom I love more than myself. O my glory and my love, may all heaven and earth be transformed into glory and love for You! Finally, I sacrifice myself all to You to be sacredly annihilated and consumed forever in the most pure fire of Your divine love.

3. O Jesus, only object of my love, with what love, with what praises can I ever repay You for all that You are in Yourself, and for all the innumerable effects of Your goodness towards all Your creatures, myself in particular? Lord, may all Your creatures, all Your angels and saints, Your Blessed Mother, and all the powers of Your divinity and humanity be employed in blessing and loving You forever.

4. O Mother of God, O holy angels, O blessed saints, I hail, honor, and thank you all in general, and each one in particular, especially those to whom I owe some special obligation and with whom I am to be most closely associated in eternity. In thanksgiving for all the favors I have received from you, and much more for all the glory and services you have rendered to my God, I offer to each one of you the most amiable heart of my Jesus, source of all joy, all glory and all praise. I

give you my mind and my heart; unite them with your minds and hearts and associate me in your constant chorus of praise to Him Who created me, that I may praise and love Him eternally with you. Pray ardently that I may bless and love Him through you, while awaiting the day when it may please Him to unite me with you to love and glorify Him to perfection.

5. O blessed day, when I shall begin to love most purely and perfectly my Lord and Savior Who is infinitely amiable! O thousand times happy day in which I shall begin to be all love for Him Who is all love for me! O Jesus, my sweet love, how consoled. I am when I think that I shall love and bless You eternally! My eyes dissolve in tears and my heart melts with joy at the sweetness of the thought that some day I shall he completely transformed into praise and love for You. Alas, when will it come, this day, so longed for and a thousand times desired? Will it yet delay for long?

"Woe is me, that my sojourning is prolonged" (see Ps. 120:5-7).

How long, O Lord, will You forget me unto the end? How long do You turn away Your face from me (Ps. 13:1)*?*

As a deer longs for running water, God, my soul longs for You. (Ps. 42:1).

No more the hunted stag desires,
fleeing in woe and weariness,
waters to quench his burning thirst,
than my poor heart with sadness pressed
sighs after You, O Lord, my rest.

My heart is driven nigh to death
By cruel desires, merciless,
And longs for You, Lord, Mighty God,
And in its longing, cries apace:
When shall my eyes behold Your face?
When, ah, when will come that day
To take my earthly woes away
And bring me home at last to You?

While waiting for that day, I desire, O my Savior, to realize in myself St. Paul's words:

"Our conversation is in heaven" (Phil. 3:20),

as well as Your words of reassurance and guidance:

"The Kingdom of God is within you" (Luke 17:21).

I desire to live on earth as though I were not here, but living by my heart and spirit in heaven. I desire to concentrate all my powers on the establishment of the Kingdom of Your glory and holy love within myself. You know, Lord, that of myself I can do nothing; therefore, I give myself to You, that You may destroy every obstacle and perfectly establish the Kingdom of Your pure love in my body, in my soul, and in all my thoughts, words, and actions.

Conclusion of the Exercise

At the end of these exercises on the subject of death, you should thank Our Lord for the graces He has given you through them and beg Him to forgive the faults you have committed in their performance. Ask Him to compensate for your deficiencies, and to accomplish in you the fulfilment of His words:

> *"Blessed is that servant, whom when his Lord shall come He shall find so doing. Amen I say to you: He shall place him over all His goods"* (Matt. 24:46-47).

Pray that He may ever watch within you and for you, lest you be taken by surprise. Beg Him to keep these exercises and preparations in store for you against the hour of your death and to be Himself your disposition and preparation.

Follow the same procedure proportionately, invoking the Blessed Virgin, the angels and saints, especially the saints on whose feast day the Lord knows you are going to die.

Some Other Points of Advice and Necessary Dispositions for a Holy Death

I shall here add a few other suggestions and practices which may prove useful to you, when you sense that your life is approaching its end.

The chief thing for you to do, when you feel that you are nearing the end of your life, is to devote yourself as much as possible to Acts of Love of Jesus, ever uniting humility with love. There is no more powerful and effective means of quickly wiping out our sins, advancing with great strides along the road to God, and giving Him pleasure than the divine exercise of active love.

If you are worried by the fear of death or by qualms of mistrust by reason of your past sins, ask some kind person to read to you the passages about confidence.

If you are not too sick to listen to reading aloud, ask some kind friend to read to you, from time to time, the foregoing meditations on death, and the exercises of praise and glorification of Jesus.

Let him also read passages from the *Lives of the Saints* or some other book of devotion, but particularly the Passion of Jesus Christ, the seventeenth chapter of the Gospel of St. John and the prayers for the agonizing soul, as on the seventh day of the "Exercise of Preparations for Death."

Do not forget, when you are at the end of your life, to remind one of your friends to gain a plenary indulgence for you, not in your own interest but for the pure glory of God, according to the method where indulgences are discussed.

Frequently clasp the Crucifix in your hands, so that you may from time to time make Acts of Love while kissing the cross and the five wounds.

Let the holy names of Jesus and Mary be ever in your heart and frequently on your lips. Renew the desire to pronounce them with the intentions recommended for the Rosary of Jesus and Mary.

Pray with St. Francis:

> "Lord, release my soul from the prison of this body that I may praise Your holy name with all the just who await me in heaven."

Constantly invoke the Blessed Virgin, using the words of Holy Church:

> O Mary, Mother of Grace, Mother of Mercy protect us from the enemy and receive us at the hour of death.

> O Mother of Jesus, be a mother to my soul.
> Show yourself my Mother.
> Show that you are the Mother of Jesus,
> by destroying in me,
> by your prayers and merits,
> all that is contrary to the Glory of your Son Jesus,
> and causing Him to be loved and glorified
> perfectly in me.

Repeat with St. Stephen:

> *"Lord Jesus, receive my spirit"* (Acts 7:59).

As you say all these words, ever unite yourself with the devotion, the love, and the other holy dispositions with which they were first pronounced.

Accept your suffering in union with Jesus, in agony in the Garden of Olives:

> *"Father, not my will, but Yours be done"* (Luke 22:42).

Again, with Jesus agonizing on the Cross, say:

> *"Father, into Your Hands I commend My Spirit"* (Luke 23:46).

Constantly lift up your heart to Jesus, saying to Him with the beloved disciple St. John:

> *"Come, Lord Jesus"* (Rev. 22:20).

Repeat with St. Peter:

"Lord, You know that I love You" (John 21:16).

Say with the good thief:

"Lord, remember me when You come into Your Kingdom" (Luke 23:42).

As you pronounce these words, unite yourself with the, heartfelt contrition of the good thief, contrition so deep and moving that he merited the infinite grace to hear from the lips of the Son of God:

"Amen I say to you: this day you shall be with Me in Paradise" (Luke 23:43).

Humbly repeat with the poor publican in the Gospel:

"O God, be merciful to me a sinner" (Luke 18:13).

Let your heart chant with King David:

"Have mercy on me, O God, according to Your great mercy" (Ps. 51:1).

"Uphold me according to Your word, and I shall live: and let me not be confounded in my expectation" (Ps. 119:116).

"In You, O Lord, have I hoped, let me never be confounded" (Ps. 31:1).

More Aspirations

You may also make use of these little aspirations:

O Jesus, love Your Father and Your Holy Spirit for me.

O Father of Jesus,
O Holy Spirit of Jesus,
O Mother of Jesus,
O angels of Jesus,
O saints of Jesus,
love Jesus for me.

Lord Jesus, I will to have You reign over me. Lord Jesus, reign over me in the midst of all Your enemies.

O my dear Jesus, be Jesus to me;

O my All be all to me, for the past, present, and future.
One thing alone is necessary.
Farewell to all things else; speak of them no more to me.

I desire but one thing,
I seek but one thing,
I love but one thing,
which is all to me,
and all else is nothing to me.

It is my sweetest Jesus Whom I desire,
my dearest Jesus Whom I seek.
Him I love
and Him I long to love with all the love
in heaven and on earth.

My Jesus is all to me.

Once more,
farewell to all that is not Jesus.
My Jesus is sufficient for me.
I desire naught but Him
in heaven and on earth.

Come Lord Jesus, enter into me,
there to love Yourself to perfection.

> O Jesus, my all,
> be, Yourself, my preparation for my death.

> O Jesus, I give myself to You
> to die with You,
> in You,
> and by You.

> O Jesus, I give myself to You
> to unite myself, at the moment of death,
> with all the dispositions
> of love and sanctity
> which ennobled the death
> of Your divine humanity,
> Your holy martyrs,
> and all the other saints.

> O Jesus,
> O Mary, Mother of Jesus,
> I implore you to give me your holy blessing.

Finally, try to make your last word he the holy name of Jesus and the sweet name of Mary:

> Jesus! Mary!

or else,

> Live Jesus!

or

> Jesus, be Jesus to me!

Thus, you may converse with Our Lord with profound devotion and consoling ease by means of frequent ejaculations. If you wish Him to give you the grace to make these loving aspirations at the hour of your death, you must develop the habit of saying these words and pronouncing these ejaculations frequently during your life, especially at night, lying in bed before falling asleep, using now one, now another, according to the inspiration of the Spirit of God.

It would also be well to ask those present around to assist you during your last sickness, to read and reread frequently the above prayers. If by chance you should lose the power of speech, let them diligently continue to make these acts on your behalf, particularly if it should happen that you lose the use of your senses or your reason. Once you have made the request and expressed to your friends that it is your will for them to make Acts of Love in your name and for you, Our Lord will accept these precious acts as if you yourself were making them, since they are made at your request and on your behalf.

Pray also to the Blessed Virgin and your special angels and saints to carry out all these things for you, together with everything else they know God expects of you on the last day of your life.

Above all, supplicate Jesus Himself to do this for you, and put great trust in His infinite goodness, that He will be your all, and will do on, your behalf everything that is required of you for a holy and happy death. I pray you to note this last point well.

Even though you should prepare yourself for death with all possible care and devotion, by means of these exercises, nonetheless, after having done all that has been suggested, you should not rely or rest upon your own acts, exercises, and preparations, but rather place all your reliance and trust in the pure goodness and mercy of our Lord Jesus Christ, ever imploring Him to be your preparation, your virtue, your sanctification, and your all.For, after all is said and done, to Jesus Christ alone does it belong to be all and accomplish all, in all men and all things that He may have the glory of all, according to the divine words of St. Paul, with which I began this book, and by which I wish to finish it:

"Christ is all and in all" (Col. 3:11).

Oh, Let Him then be all, in time and in eternity!

O Jesus be all.
Be all on earth as You are in heaven.
Be all in all men and things.
Be all in this little book.
Everything it has of good is all from You.
It speaks but of You and for You;

it aims only at forming and establishing You
in the souls of those who use it.
Let its readers see in it nothing but Jesus,
seek in it nothing but Jesus,
and learn from it nothing
but to love and glorify Jesus.
Be all to him who has written this book
and to those who shall read it;
for You know,
O Jesus, my dear all,
that it is my will never, in life or in death,
to have any other object or desire
but to see You live and reign in all men
and all things.

Live then, Jesus, live and reign in us.

The pitiable crowd cried:

"We will not have this Man to reign over us."

We, on the contrary, desire to proclaim in the face of heaven
and on earth:

"We want You, Lord Jesus, to reign over us."

Reign, therefore, O King of souls, dwell perfectly and
absolutely in Your Kingdom in our hearts that we may forever
sing the divine canticle:

"Jesus is all in all things!"
Live Jesus! Live
You great all!
Live great Jesus,
Who are all!
Live this great all,
which is Jesus!
Live Jesus!
Live Jesus!

LIVE JESUS AND MARY

ENDING THE DAY WITH JESUS

Ending the Day with Jesus

It is just as important to end as it is to begin the day well and to make a special consecration to God of the last actions of each day as well as the first. To this end, before taking your rest in the evening, make a point of going on your knees for a quarter of an hour to thank God for the graces He has given you during the day, to examine your conscience and to renew the offering of yourself to Him by the following exercises and practices.

Act of Thanksgiving

O Jesus, my Lord, I adore You as the One who, together with Your Father and Your Holy Spirit, are the source of all that is good and holy and perfect in heaven and on earth, in the orders of nature, of grace, and of glory. To You do I refer all the gifts and benefits, both earthly and heavenly, temporal and eternal, which ever came forth from You, but especially this day, both on earth and in heaven.

I give You infinite praise and thanks for all that You are in Yourself, and for all the effects of Your goodness that You have ever brought about, especially during this day, for the benefit of all Your creatures.

I thank You more especially for those You have accomplished for me, the most insignificant of Your creatures, as well as for all the benefits You have designed on my behalf from all eternity.

I offer You all the love and all the praises that have ever been given You, especially all those that have been given You today in heaven and on earth. May all the angels, all the saints, all creatures and all powers of Your divinity and Your humanity bless You forever.

Examination of Conscience

O Lord Jesus, I adore You as my sovereign judge. Most willingly do I submit to Your power of judging me and I rejoice that You have this power over me. May it please You to let me share a little of that light by which You will show me my sins, when I appear before Your judgment seat at the hour of death, so that, in the brightness of that light, I may know the sins I have committed against your divine majesty. Let me share in the zeal of Your divine justice and in Your hatred for sin, so that I may hate my sins as You hate them.

Having said this prayer, make a brief examination of the whole day to see whether you have offended God. When you have recalled your sins, accuse yourself before Him and ask pardon of Him, making use of the following acts of contrition.

Act of Contrition Before Retiring

O my Savior, I accuse myself before You and before all Your angels and saints, of all the sins that I have committed in my whole life, especially today, against Your divine majesty. I implore You, my Lord, by Your great mercy, by the precious blood which You shed for me and by the prayers and merits of Your most holy Mother and of all Your angels and saints, to give me grace, at this time, to conceive true contrition and repentance for my sins.

O my God, I detest my sins with my whole heart and with all the power of my will. I detest them because of the offense, injury, and dishonor which I have given You by means of them. I hate them because You hate them and because they are infinitely displeasing to You. O good Jesus, these sins of mine have been the reason for which You suffered the most frightful tortures that have ever been suffered, and You died the most cruel of all deaths. That is why I hold them in abhorrence, O my good Savior, and renounce them forever. O who will give me all the anguish of St. Peter or St. Mary Magdalen and all the penitent saints, that I may weep for the offenses I have committed against my God with all the feeling and all the regret with which they wept for theirs! O who will bring me to hate all my iniquities as much as the angels and saints hate them!

O my God, if it were only possible for me to have as great a horror for my sins as You have Yourself! Lord, let me detest them, let me hold them in abhorrence even as You do and let me loathe all that is not pleasing to You!

O my sweet Lord, let me die a thousand times rather than offend You mortally again, or, indeed, rather than offend You in any way at all, by a deliberate act of will. I promise, with the help of Your grace, that I will accuse myself of all my sins at my next confession and I assure You of my firm resolution to avoid them in the future for love of You. Yes, my God, with my whole heart, I renounce every sort of sin forever and I offer myself to You to do and to suffer all You please, in satisfaction for my sins. In homage to Your divine justice, I now willingly accept all the sufferings and penances it shall please You to inflict upon me, whether in this world or in the next, in expiation of my faults, to satisfy for the dishonor I have given You today by Yourself, Your holy Mother, by Your angels and saints and by all the holy souls there are on earth.

O good Jesus, I give myself all to You. Destroy in me all that does not please You. Make reparation, on my behalf, for all the offenses I have committed before Your Eternal Father, Yourself, Your Holy Spirit, Your Blessed Mother, Your angels, Your saints, and all Your creatures. Give me the strength and grace to offend You no more.

O angels of Jesus, saints of Jesus, Mother of Jesus, make up for my defects, I beg you; atone on my behalf for the dishonor I have given God by my sins, and return to Him a hundredfold all the honor and glory I should have given Him today and in my whole life.

O Mother of Jesus, Mother of Mercy, ask your beloved Son to show me His mercy. Mother of Grace, implore your Son to give me grace never to offend Him again and to serve and love Him faithfully.

O blessed St. Joseph, O my Guardian Angel, O blessed St. John and blessed St. Mary Magdalen, intercede for me that I may obtain mercy and grace to be more faithful to God.

Act of Oblation

O Jesus, I offer You the rest I am about to take, in honor of the eternal rest You enjoy in the bosom of Your Father, and in honor of the sleep and temporal rest You took in the bosom of Your Mother, as well as during Your whole life on earth.

I offer You every breath I shall draw during this night, every pulse of my heart and my veins, desiring that they may be so many acts of praise and adoration of You. I unite myself with all the praises which will be offered up to You, this night and forever, in heaven and on earth.

I beg all Your angels and saints, Your Blessed Mother and Your very Self to love and glorify You for me this night and for all eternity.

When you have said this and are lying down, you should make the sign of the Cross. Then say the last prayer that Jesus said to His Father at the last moment of His life:

"Father, into Your hands I commend my spirit" (Luke 23:46).

You should say this prayer with your life's last hour in view and try to say it with just as much devotion as you would wish if you were indeed in that last hour. To do this, you must desire to make the offering, as far as possible, with the love, the humility, the confidence, and all the divine and holy dispositions with which Jesus said these words Himself. At the same time unite yourself, as of that moment, with the final disposition in which Jesus ended His life, saying this prayer and imploring Him to impress those dispositions deeply within you and to keep them there for you in your last hour, so that, by this means, you may die in Christ, that is, in the holy and divine dispositions in which he died, and thus you may be one of those of whom it is written:

"Blessed are the dead who die in the Lord" (Rev. 14:13).

Finally, take care that your last action before falling asleep is the Sign of the Cross; and that your last thought is of Jesus, that your last inward act is an Act of Love for Jesus and Mary. Thus, you may merit the grace that the last words you say in your life will be these:

Jesus!
Mary!
Live Jesus and Mary!
O good Jesus, be Jesus to me!
O Mary, Mother of Jesus, be the mother of my soul!

Ending the Year
with Jesus

Ending the Year with Jesus

To end each year of your life with Jesus, you ought to close it just as Jesus ended His mortal, human life on earth. You ought to set aside a little time at the end of each year to acquit yourself of your obligations and offer fitting homage to Jesus as the following prayer suggests.

Prayer of Praise and Gratitude for the Close of the Year.

O Jesus, my Lord, I adore, love and glorify You in the last day, the last hour and last minute of Your mortal life on earth. I adore all that happened both inwardly and outwardly on that last day, I mean, Your last thoughts, acts, words and sufferings, Your final use of the senses of Your sacred body, and the last dispositions of Your holy soul, to which I desire to unite myself now, with a view to the closing moment of my own life.

O divine Jesus, by the light of faith I behold You on that last day of your life, adoring and loving Your Father infinitely. You give Him fitting thanks for all the graces imparted to You and, through You, to the whole world during the time of Your sojourn on earth. You ask His pardon for all the sins of men, offering Yourself to Him to suffer the penance due to them. You think of me with exceeding great love, with a most ardent desire to draw me to Yourself. Finally You sacrifice Your precious blood and Your most noble life, for the glory of the heavenly Father and for love of us. Blessed be You infinitely for all these inestimable graces.

O good Jesus, in honor of and in union with the love, humility, and other holy dispositions with which You performed all the last actions of Your life, I give You infinite thanks for all the glory You gave the Eternal Father during Your life on earth, for all the graces You have bestowed upon me and all men this year and always, as well as for the graces You would have lavished on me, if I had not stood in Your way.

I most humbly beg Your forgiveness for all the outrages and indignities You suffered on earth because of me, and for all the offenses I have committed against You this year. In satisfaction, I offer You all the honor and glory rendered to You, during Your Time on earth and during the past year, by Your Eternal Father, the Holy Spirit, Your holy Mother, and by all the angels and saints. So, too, I offer myself to You to bear all the penance You may ordain for me in this world and in the next.

O Jesus, most worthy of love, I adore Your infinite thoughts and designs for me on the last day of Your most precious life; and I give myself to You to do and suffer all You desire of me, for the fulfilment of these unfathomable designs. Grant that I may die a thousand times rather than hinder the operation of Your loving providence.

O good Jesus, I offer to You the last day, the last hour, and the last moment of my life and everything that may happen to me outwardly and inwardly then. I mean, my last thoughts, words, actions, and sufferings, as well as the last use of my bodily senses and of the powers of my soul.

May it please You to grant that all these things may be consecrated to the honor of the last day, the last hour and last moment of Your life. May I die loving You with Your holy love. May my being and my life be sacrificed and consumed for Your glory, and may my last breath be an act of pure love of You. This is my intention, my desire, my expectation. O my dear Jesus, relying as I do upon the excess of your infinite love, may it please You to grant, by Your great mercy that this may be so.

Prayer to the Blessed Virgin, at the End of the Year

O Mother of Jesus, Mother of the eternal and immortal God made Man, I honor and venerate you in the last hour and moment of your life. I honor your last thoughts, words, and acts, and the last use made of the senses of your immaculate body and of the powers of your glorious soul. Especially I wish to honor the last Act of Love made by your mother's heart for your most beloved Son.

With all my heart I bless and thank you, O holy Virgin, for all the glory you rendered to God during your spotless life, and for all the graces you ever obtained from His bounty for me and for all men, especially during this year.

I beg your forgiveness, O Mother of Mercy, for all the offenses you suffered on earth, as well as for those I have committed this year against you. To make satisfaction for these, I offer you all the honor that has ever been accorded you in heaven and on earth.

O Mother of Fair Love, I offer you the last day, the last hour, and moment of my life, and all that shall take place in me at that last moment, in honor of the last moment, hour, and day of your life, and of all that occurred in you on that day. Unite me, if it please you, with all the holy and divine dispositions of your maternal heart and your pure soul. Grant that, by your merits and prayers, my last thoughts, words, acts, and breaths may be consecrated to the honor of the last thought, words, acts, and breaths, both of your Son and of yourself. Grant that I may die loving Him with His holy love, and that I may be utterly consumed and sacrificed to His glory, and that my life may end with a last act of most pure love for Him. O angels and saints of Christ, pray that He may consummate all this in me, by His exceeding great mercy and for love of Him.

Annual Confession

Once you have made a good general confession, you should no longer think of your past sins, that is, not consider and examine them in detail any more, but be satisfied to detest them in general and humble yourself before God for them. It is, however, a very profitable thing, and a most important one, to make an annual confession, to review the chief faults you have committed during each year. For it is much to be feared that you may have frequently been remiss in your ordinary confessions, by having failed to approach the tribunal with the necessary preparation, contrition and other dispositions demanded by the sacrament of Penance. You cannot be too careful or diligent in a matter so important as the salvation of a soul created to love and glorify God forever.

Yearly confession has become a frequent practice among all Christians who desire to please God and to guarantee their salvation for the glory of God. There are many, indeed, who review their confessions every six months, and still others at even shorter intervals.

Adopt this holy practice at least at the end of each year, so that you may to some extent repair your failings during the year and dispose yourself to serve and love God more perfectly the next year. If you do not do this at the end of the year, make your review of your confessions at some other time, according to the advice of your confessor, but in any case, perform it with an unusual amount of preparation, self-abasement and contrition.

Above all, make a point of protesting to Our Lord that you do not wish to make this exercise for the unburdening and satisfaction of your soul, nor for your own merit or interest, but solely for His pleasure and pure glory.

Confession

Preparation for Confession

The frequent use of the sacrament of Penance is a very useful, holy and necessary means for the glory of God and the sanctification of souls. It is a deplorable thing to see what a strange abuse many souls make of this sacrament in our own day, when they come to the feet of the priest to receive absolution for their sins but get up and bear away their own condemnation because they have come without the dispositions necessary for true and solid repentance. This is a matter to be feared extremely, even by those who confess frequently, because there is a real danger of their going to confession more as a matter of routine than in a real spirit of penance, especially when they can detect no change in their life and no progress in Christian virtues. Therefore, the more you frequent this sacrament, the more you should see that you make the proper preparation for receiving it. There are three things that will enable you to do, so.

1. You must fall on your knees before Our Lord, in some quiet place, if possible, to consider Him and adore Him in the rigorous penances, in the contrition and humiliation which he had to bear for your sins all through His life, especially in the Garden of Olives. You should beg Him with great insistence to let you share in His spirit of penance, and to give you the grace to know your sins, to hate and detest them as much as He would wish, to confess them clearly, to give them up absolutely, and to be converted perfectly to Him, flying from all occasions of sin, while making use of the remedies necessary for the healing of the wounds of your soul.

   To do this, you may use the following prayer:

   > O my dear Jesus, as I contemplate You in the Garden of Olives when You entered upon Your sacred passion, I behold You prostrate upon the ground before Your Father's face in the name of all sinners, since You have taken upon Yourself all the sins of the world and,

62

especially, my own. I see that by Your divine light You place all those sins before Your own gaze, to confess them to Your Father in the name of all sinners, taking upon Yourself all the humiliation and contrition for them in His sight, and offering Yourself to Him to make whatever satisfaction and perform whatever penance is pleasing to Him.

O my good Jesus, I behold You, as a result of this spectacle of the horror of my crimes and of the dishonor they give to Your Father, reduced to an astounding agony, a frightful sorrow, and to such an extremity of anguish and contrition, that the violence of the suffering makes Your soul sorrowful unto death and causes You even to sweat blood, so terribly as to stain the ground about You.

O my Savior, I adore, love, and glorify You in Your holy agony and in this spirit of penance to which You have been reduced by Your love and my offenses. I give myself to You now, that I may enter with You into this spirit. May it please You to give me some little share of the light that gave You cognizance of my faults, that I may know them and confess them humbly. Give me some small share of the humiliation and contrition You bore before the Eternal Father, as well as some measure of the love with which You offered Yourself to Him in atonement and some fraction of Your hatred and horror for sin. Give me the grace, I beseech You, to make this confession with perfect humility, sincerity and repentance and with a firm and strong resolution never to offend You again.

O Mother of Jesus, I implore You to obtain for me those graces from your Son.

O my holy Guardian Angel, pray to Our Lord for me, to give me the grace to know my sins and confess them well, and to have true contrition for them and to be perfectly converted from them.

2. When you have said this prayer, you should examine your
    conscience with care and try to remember the sins you
    have committed since your last confession. Once you have
    recognized them, try to form in your heart real regret,
    perfect repentance, and contrition for having offended so
    good a God, asking Him pardon for your faults, detesting
    them and renouncing them because they displease Him,
    making a firm resolution to avoid them in the future, with
    the help of His grace, flying from all occasions of sin, and
    making use of the proper and efficacious means to bring
    about a genuine conversion: for contrition is composed of
    all these elements.

    Since, however, contrition is extremely necessary and
    important, not only in confession but in several other
    matters as well, I should like to show you in more detail the
    nature of contrition, and when and how you ought to make
    Acts of Contrition. This will be done after I have told you
    the third thing necessary for a perfect confession and what
    to do after you have confessed.

3. The third thing you must do, if you want to make a perfect
    confession, is to kneel before the priest as before one who
    represents the Person of Jesus Christ and takes His place.
    Present yourself to him as a criminal who has outraged the
    majesty of God, with the full intention of humiliating and
    confounding yourself, taking God's side against yourself,
    as against His enemy which you are in so far as you are a
    sinner, and being ready to arm yourself with His zeal for
    justice against sin and His infinite hatred for it.

    Do, not fail to bring with you the firm resolve to confess
    your sins humbly, completely and clearly, without disguises,
    without excuses, and without trying to shift the blame on to
    somebody else. Rather accuse yourself as though you were
    on the point of death. For it would be well to reflect that it
    is far better to state your sins in the ear of the priest than to
    bear the shame of them on the day of judgment, before the
    entire world, and then be damned forever.

    Remember that you ought to be willing to accept with
    cheerfulness and courage the pain and confusion that go

with the confession of sins, out of homage for the confusion and torments suffered by our Lord Jesus Christ upon the Cross for those very same sins, as well as to glorify Our Lord by your humiliations, remembering that the more you abase yourself, the more He is exalted in you.

Thanksgiving After Confession

After you have confessed your sins and received pardon for them through the sacrament of Penance, do not forget to thank Our Lord for having given you so great a grace. When He delivers you from some great sin, either by preventing you from failing into it, or by pardoning you after your fall, even if it is only the smallest venial sin in the world, He is giving you a greater grace, for which You owe Him more thanks, than if He had preserved you from all the plagues, diseases, and other afflictions of the body that might beset you. Therefore, thank Him in such words as these, praying Him to preserve you from sin in the future.

> Be You blessed, O good Jesus, be blessed a thousand times! May all Your angels and Your saints and Your holy Mother bless You now and forever, for having established in Your Church the holy sacrament of Penance and for having given us so accessible, so easy and so efficacious a means of wiping out our sins and becoming reconciled with You! Be blessed for all the glory that has been and will be given You by this sacrament until the end of the world! Blessed be You, also, for all the glory You have Yourself rendered to Your Father by the confession, if one may say such a thing, which You made to Him of our sins, in the Garden of Olives and by the humiliation, contrition, and penance You bore for them! O my Savior, engrave deep within me a great hatred, abhorrence and fear of sin, greater than all the other evils on earth and in hell and let me die a thousand deaths rather than offend You again.

Nature of Contrition

Contrition is so powerful, so holy and so desirable that a single act of true contrition is capable of wiping out a thousand mortal sins, if they were to be found in the soul.

Contrition is an act of hatred and abhorrence, of sorrow and repentance at the sight of a sin you have committed, because this sin offends God. It is an act of the will, by which you tell God that you desire to hate and detest your sins, that you are filled with shame for having committed them, and that you renounce them earnestly, not for your own interests but because of His. By this I mean, not so much because of the evil, injury and harm you have done to yourself, but because of the dishonor, great sufferings and most cruel death you have caused Our Lord to suffer by your sins.

It is true that the very slightest offense against the infinite goodness of God is so detestable that even if you were to weep until the Day of Judgment, or even if you were to die of grief over the smallest of your faults, it would not be enough. Nevertheless, in order to have contrition it is not absolutely necessary to shed tears, nor to conceive a pain that can be felt, nor a sensible feeling of anguish over our sins. Contrition is an interior and spiritual act of the will which is a spiritual power and not a faculty of sense; therefore, you may make an Act of Contrition without any sensible pain. It is enough to assure Our Lord, with the real will to carry out what you promise, that you want to hate and detest your sins, and to avoid them in the future, because they displease Him, and that you shall confess them at your next confession.

It should also be remembered that contrition is a gift of God and an effect of grace. Even if you had perfect knowledge of its essence and applied all the strength of your mind and will to make an Act of Contrition, you would never be able to do so if the Holy Spirit did not give you grace. You may console yourself with the thought that this grace will never be refused if you ask for it with humility, confidence and perseverance, and if you do not wait until the hour of your death to ask for it. For grace is ordinarily refused, in that last hour, to those who have neglected it during their lifetime.

Notice, also, that four things are necessary for true contrition.

The first of these is to make restitution, at the earliest possible opportunity of things belonging to others, if you have anything that it is possible to return; also, to restore the good name of another when you have robbed him of it by calumny or backbiting.

The second thing is to do everything in your power to bring about reconciliation with those with whom you are at odds.

The third is to have a firm and constant will, not only to confess your sins and renounce them, but also to use the necessary remedies and means to overcome evil habits, and to begin to live a truly Christian life.

The fourth thing is effectively to give up all active and passive occasions of sin — that is, the occasions you give others to offend God, as well as those by which you yourself are led into sin. Such occasions are, for instance: for the promiscuously impure and the adulterous, their partners in evil; for drunkards, their taverns; for gamblers and blasphemers, their games, when they have the habit of swearing and blaspheming or losing very much time and money at these pastimes; women and girls should avoid the least thing that tends to immodesty in dress, as well as excessive novelty and vanity in the matter of fashions; others should give up bad books, improper pictures, the wrong kind of parties and shows, and avoid certain groups, or certain individuals, as well as certain occupations which lead them into sin.

The Son of God Himself says:

> *"If your hand, or your foot scandalizes you, cut it off, and cast it from you. It is better for you to go into life maimed or lame, than having two hands or two feet, to be cast into hell fire. And if your eye scandalizes you, pluck it out, and cast it from you. It is better for you having one eye to enter into life, than having two eyes to be cast into hell fire"* (Matt. 18:8-9).

He is giving you here an absolute commandment under pain of eternal damnation (as the Holy Fathers explain these words of Sacred Scripture), to cut off from yourself and entirely renounce all things that are occasions of ruin for yourself and others, even those which are not in themselves evil, even occupations and professions, if you cannot follow them without sinning, as well as things that are most close and dear and precious to you, if these things might occasion the loss of your soul.

Acts of Contrition may be made at all times and in every situation, but they should be made particularly at such times as:

1. When you go to Confession, for perfect contrition or at the very least attrition, which is imperfect contrition, is a necessary part of Penance. That is why I said above and here repeat, that, before you go to Confession and after your Examination of Conscience, you should ask God for contrition and then try to make genuine Acts of Sorrow for sin.

2. When you have fallen into sin, so that you may instantly rise again by means of contrition.

3. In the morning and evening, so that if you have committed any sins during the night or in the day, they may be wiped out by contrition, and so you may always remain in God's grace. For this cause, I have set down various Acts of Contrition in the Evening Exercise, following the Examination of Conscience.

   Over and above this, to give you readier access to the means and method of practicing so necessary and important a virtue, which you need at every moment of your life, I have also added several varied Acts of Contrition which you may use, taking now one, now another, according to the promptings and guidance of the Spirit of God.

   However, do not make the mistake of imagining that, in order to have contrition for your sins, it is sufficient to read and pronounce with attention the acts set down in this book, or others like them. True contrition must be accompanied by the conditions described above, but you must also remember in particular that you cannot make a single Act of Contrition without a special grace from God. Therefore, when you want to have true repentance and contrition for your faults, be sure to pray Our Lord to give you grace to do so.

Prayer to Beg God for Contrition

O Good Jesus, I desire to have all the contrition and repentance for my faults that You desire me to have. Yet You know that I can not have this unless You give it to me. Grant me contrition, I beg You, O my Savior, in Your great mercy. I know that I am unworthy that You should look upon me and hear my prayer, but I trust in Your infinite bounty, believing that You will give me what I ask of You most fervently, through the merits of Your holy passion, of Your holy Mother and of all Your angels and saints.

O Mother of Jesus, O holy angels and blessed saints, pray to Jesus for me that He may give me perfect repentance for my sins.

After this prayer strive to make earnest Acts of Pure Contrition:

Acts of Contrition

O my Most Amiable Jesus, I hate and detest my sins for love of You.

O my Savior, I renounce all sin forever because it offends You.

O my Jesus, I abhor my offenses because of the insult and dishonor I have given You by them.

O my God, would that I had never offended You, for You are so worthy of honor and love.

O my Lord, I desire to have all the contrition You will me to have for my sins.

O my God, would that I had in my heart all the sorrow and contrition possessed by all the penitent saints.

O Good Jesus, make me share the sorrow which You Yourself bore for my sins. I desire to have the greatest possible measure of the same contrition that You bore.

O Father of Jesus, I offer up to You and unite myself with the contrition and penance that Your well-beloved Son felt for my sins.

O most amiable Jesus, may I hate and detest my sins because they were the cause of Your torments and Your dreadful death on the Cross.

O my God, I want to hate my sins as vehemently as Your angels and saints hate them.

O my God, I desire to hate and detest my sins with the same hatred with which You hate and detest them Yourself.,

You might also make an Act of Contrition by striking your breast like the poor publican in the Gospel and saying with him:

"O God, be merciful to me a sinner" (Luke 18:13).

You must desire to do and say this with the same contrition that the publican had, by virtue of which he went down to his house justified, as we are told by the Son of God Himself.

These are a few Acts of Contrition, which are capable of wiping out all sorts of sins, provided only that they he uttered, either with the lips or in the heart, with a real will prompted by the workings of grace, and with a firm resolve to abandon sin and the occasions of sin, and to confess it, and carry out [at the earliest possible opportunity] all the other conditions mentioned above.

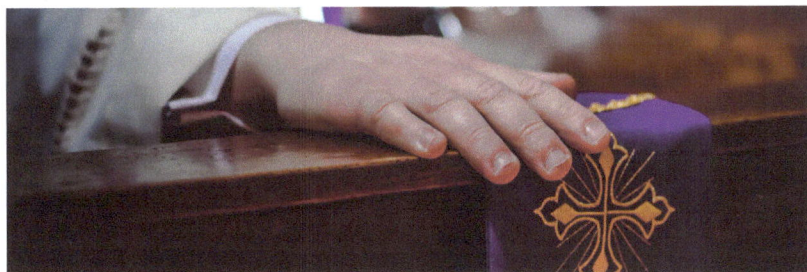

Holy Communion

Preparation for Holy Communion

Our Lord Jesus Christ comes to you in the blessed Eucharist, with the greatest humility, abasing Himself so far as to take the form and appearance of bread, to give Himself to you, and with the most ardent love that impels Him to give you, in this sacrament, all the greatest, most dear, and most precious things He has. You also should receive Him in this same sacrament with the deepest humility and the greatest love.

These are the two principal dispositions you should have when you go to holy Communion.

Prayer Before Holy Communion

O Jesus, my light and my sanctification, open the eyes of my spirit and fill my soul with Your grace, so that I may realize the importance of the action I am about to perform, and do it in a holy and worthy manner for Your glory.

O my soul, I pray you, consider attentively how great and marvelous is the action you are about to perform and how great is the holiness and dignity of Him Whom you are about to receive. You are about to partake of the greatest, most important, holiest, and most divine action you could ever perform. You are about to receive on your tongue, in your breast, and in the most intimate recesses of yourself, your God, your sovereign Lord and your Savior. Yes, you are about to receive, really and actually, Jesus Himself in His own person, who lives for all eternity in the bosom of His Father; Jesus Himself, who is the life, the glory, the riches, the love and the delight of the Eternal Father; the very same Jesus Whom so many patriarchs, prophets and just men of the Old Testament desired to see; the same Jesus who dwelt nine months in the womb of the Blessed Virgin Whom she nursed and carried so often in her arms; the same Jesus Who was seen walking and living on the earth, eating and drinking with sinners; the same Jesus

Who was nailed to the cross. You are about to receive the same body that was bruised and torn and shattered for love of you; the same blood that was shed upon the ground. You are about to receive next to your own heart the very heart Which was pierced by a lance. You are about to receive in your soul the soul of Jesus, which, when dying on the cross, He commended into the hands of His Father. What a miracle of wonder! To think that I should receive into myself the very same Savior Who ascended in glory and triumph into heaven, Who sits at God's right hand, and will come in power and majesty at the end of time to judge the universe.

O most great, most admirable Jesus, the angels purer than the sun do not esteem themselves worthy to look upon You, to praise You and to adore You; and today You not only allow me to contemplate You, You even desire me to take You into my heart and soul so that I may then have within myself all dvinity, all of the most holy Trinity and all Paradise. Ah, my Lord, what goodness is this! Whence comes this happiness to me, that the sovereign King of heaven and earth should desire to take up his abode in me, who am a hell of wretchedness and sin, in order to change me into a paradise of graces and blessings? O my God, how unworthy I am of such a favor! For I do indeed avow, in the presence of heaven and earth, that I deserve by far rather to be cast into the bottom most depths of hell, than to receive You into my soul, so full of vices and imperfections.

Yet since it pleases You, O my Savior, to give Yourself to me in this way, I desire to receive You with all possible purity and love and devotion. With this intention, O good Jesus, I give You my soul. Prepare me as You Yourself desire. Destroy in me everything that is contrary to You, fill me with Your divine love and with all the other graces and dispositions with which You will me to receive You.

O Father of Jesus; annihilate in me everything that is displeasing to Your Son and impart to me a share of Your love for Him, with which You received Him into Your paternal bosom on the day of the Ascension.

O Holy Spirit of Jesus, I offer You my soul; adorn it with all the graces and virtues necessary to receive our Savior.

O Mother of my God, may it please you to let me share the faith and devotion, love and humility, the purity and sanctity with which you so often received Communion after your Son's Ascension.

O holy angels and blessed saints, to you also, do I offer my soul. Offer it to my Jesus and pray Him to make it ready Himself, and that He may allow me to share in your purity and holiness, and in the very great love you bear for Him.

O my Dear Jesus, I offer You all the humility and devotion, all the purity and sanctity, all the love and all the preparation with which You have ever been received by the holy souls that are, and ever have been, on the earth. Would that I had in myself the holy fervor, the divine love of all the angels, of all the seraphim, of all the saints on earth and in heaven, in order the more worthily to receive You. O my sweet love, You are all love for me in the sacrament of love and You come to me with an infinite love. Alas, why am I not also all love for You, that I might receive You into a soul entirely transformed into love for You.

Yet, O my Lord, nothing is worthy of You but Your own Self, and there is no love by which You could be worthily received, except Your own divine love. Therefore, in order to receive You, not into myself, as being too unworthy of such a thing, but into Your own self, with the love which You have for Yourself, I reduce to nothingness before You both myself and all that is mine. I give myself to You; I beg You to take up Your abode in me, and to establish in me Your divine love, so that when You come to me in holy Communion, You may be received not into me, but into Yourself, with all the love with which You love Yourself.

Take special note of the last part of this prayer, for in it is to be found the true disposition with which we are to receive the Son of God in holy Communion. I have placed it here at the end for the benefit of more spiritual and more advanced souls. Notice also that it is by no means useless to desire to have in you all the devotion and love of all holy souls, because Our Lord revealed to St. Mechtilde, a nun of the holy Order of St. Benedict, that if, when she went to Communion, she did not feel any devotion in herself, she should desire to have the devotion and the love of all the holy souls who had ever received Communion and He would consider her as if she did indeed possess it.

We also read of St. Gertrude, a contemporary of St. Mechtilde, a member of the same order and of the same monastery, that one day, when she was about to receive Communion, and did not feel herself to be as well prepared or as full of devotion as she desired, she turned to Our Lord and offered Him all the preparation and devotion of all the saints and of the Blessed Virgin. The result of this was that He appeared to her and spoke to her the following words:

> "Now indeed You do appear in My sight, and in the sight of my saints, clad in just those garments and ornaments that you have desired!"

Ah, Lord, how good You are thus to accept our good desires as real effects!

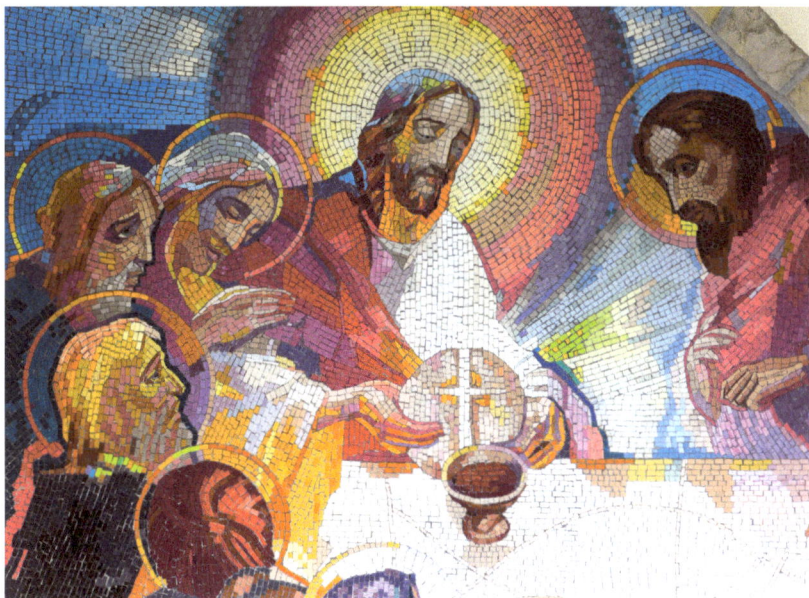

Thanksgiving After Holy Communion

There are three things you should do after holy Communion:

1. You should prostrate yourself in spirit at the feet of the Son of God abiding within you, to adore Him and ask His pardon for all your sins and ingratitude and for having received Him into so unworthy a place, with so little love and so poorly disposed.

2. You must thank Him for having given Himself to you, and in invite all things in heaven and on the earth to bless Him with you.

3. Since He has given Himself all to you, you should give yourself all to Him, and beg Him to destroy in you everything that is contrary to Him and to establish in you forever the empire of His love and glory.

Prayer After Holy Communion

O Jesus, O my God and my Creator, my sovereign Lord, what marvel is this? That I should truly, at this very moment, possess in my heart the One who resides eternally in the bosom of the Father! That I should indeed bear within me the same Jesus Whom the most holy Virgin bore within her pure womb! That the most amiable heart of Jesus, upon which the well-beloved disciple rested, which was pierced by the lance upon the cross, should truly rest in me, so close to my heart! That His most holy soul should be living in my own soul! That the divinity, the most holy Trinity, all that is most admirable in God and in heaven should have become merged in me, a most insignificant and most unworthy creature! O God, what mercies, what favors are these! What can I say, what can I do when I behold such great and astonishing marvels?

Ah, my Lord Jesus, let all the powers of my soul and body prostrate themselves before Your divine majesty to adore You and render You fitting homage! May heaven and earth, and all the creatures that are in heaven and on earth come now and cast themselves at Your feet that, with me,

76

they may render to You a thousand acts of homage and adoration! But, O my God, how great is my boldness, that I should receive You, the Saint of saints, into so vile an abode, with so little love, so little preparation! Forgive me, my Savior; with all my heart I beg forgiveness for this as well as for all the other sins and acts of ingratitude during my past life.

O most gentle and amiable Jesus, O You the only One of my heart, O well-beloved of my soul, O object of all my affections, O my sweet life, my dear soul, my one and only love, my treasure and my glory, my joy and my only hope! My Jesus, what am I to think of Your bounties, so exceedingly great to me? What am I to do for Your love, when You have wrought so many wonders for me? What thanks can I give You? My Savior, I offer You all the blessings that ever have been and ever will be given You for all eternity by Your Father, Your Holy Spirit, Your holy Mother, by all Your angels and by all the holy souls who have ever received You in holy Communion.

My God, may all that is in me be transformed into love and praise of You! May Your Father, Your Holy Spirit, all Your angels, Your saints, and all Your creatures bless You eternally for me! Father of Jesus, Holy Spirit of Jesus, Mother of Jesus, angels of Jesus, saints of Jesus, bless Jesus for me!

O good Jesus, You have given Yourself to me with a love most great. In this same love I give myself to You. I give You my body, my soul, my life, my thoughts, my words, and my deeds, and all that depends upon me. I give myself all to You, that You may dispose of me and of all that belongs to me, in time and in eternity, according to Your most adorable will. O my Lord and my God, make use, Yourself, of the power of your own hand to ravish me from myself, from the world and from all that is not Yourself, that You may entirely possess me. Destroy all my self-love, my own will and all my vices and unruly desires. Establish in my soul the Kingdom of Your pure love, of Your holy glory and of Your divine will, so that I may henceforth love You perfectly. And let me love nothing, except in You and for You.

May all my pleasure be in pleasing You, all my glory in glorifying You and in leading others to give You glory. May my most perfect happiness consist in carrying out Your holy desires. O good Jesus, establish in me the reign of Your humility, Your charity, Your gentleness and patience, Your obedience, Your modesty, Your chastity and all Your other virtues. Clothe me in Your spirit, Your thoughts and inclinations, so that I may no longer have any thoughts, desires, or inclinations except Your own. Finally, annihilate everything in me that is opposed to You, and so in me love and glorify Yourself in all the ways You desire.

O my Savior, I offer You all the persons for whom I am bound to pray, and especially N.N. . . . Destroy in them all that is displeasing to You. Fill them with Your divine love. Accomplish all the plans of Your divine goodness for their souls, and give to them everything that I have asked for myself.

Preparation to Gain Indulgence

At frequent intervals during the course of the year, rich opportunities for gaining indulgences are available; yet most Christians are satisfied to seek nothing more on such occasions than exemption from dire punishment due to their sins, having practically no other end in view but their own interest. This very fact prevents many from gaining the desired indulgences and robs God of the glory which constitutes the purpose for which He offered them to you. it will consequently be very much to the point if I give you some idea of the intentions and dispositions you ought to have, if you are to gain indulgences worthily for the pure glory of God. Hence, when you wish to gain an indulgence, prepare yourself accordingly.

1. Adore the very great love which prompts God to grant you these indulgences. His burning love for you gives Him a very great desire to behold you soon united with Him; and as He well knows that the punishments you have deserved by your sins will defer the fulfillment of His desires, by detaining you in Purgatory, unless wiped out in this world, He wills to give you indulgences, which are the shortest and easiest way of wiping out your deserved punishment. Give yourself to Him, in order to gain a wealth of precious indulgences not so much out of consideration for your own interests, as to fulfill His constant desire to bring you nearer to Him. Carry out everything prescribed for gaining the indulgences, in honor of and in union with the most pure love that prompts God to give them to you.

2. Adore the exceeding great love of Jesus, by which He acquired these indulgences. You must see them as fruits of the cross and Passion of Christ, as graces which cost Him dearly indeed, since He purchased them at the price of His blood and death. Hence, you should desire to gain indulgences so that the Son of God may not he cheated of the fruits and effects of His cross, and in order that what cost Him so dearly may not be lost, nor become vain and fruitless so far as you are concerned.

3. Adore God's justice, before which you are accountable for the penalties due to your sins, and cultivate an active desire to gain indulgences, not to escape those penalties, but to satisfy and glorify God's justice.

4. It is also good to adore God's universal design for your soul from all eternity. For from all eternity God designs to establish you in a high degree of grace on earth and of glory in heaven. However, by your sins, you have put many obstacles in the way of the fulfillment of His eternal plan. Even though the guilt of your sins may have been forgiven by a good confession, you have, nevertheless, made yourself unworthy to receive many of the graces God designed to give you, if you had not prevented Him by your sins. Now, He desires by indulgences to wipe out these iniquities and remove from your heart the obstacles raised by sin against the fulfilment of His plans. He wishes to make you capable and worthy to receive the graces planned for you in accomplishment of His infinite designs. Desire, therefore, again these indulgences not to escape the sufferings; of Purgatory, but that God may avoid being disappointed in the designs He deigns to entertain in your regard.

5. Desire to gain indulgences so that your souls may be perfectly cleansed of many evil effects left by sin, which prevent you from loving God perfectly, thus you may become able to love Him with a more pure and ardent love. To do this, each time some opportunity of gaining an indulgence arises, address the Son of God as follows:

> O Jesus, I give myself to You to do all that You desire me to do in order to gain this indulgence, in honor of and in union with the very great love with which You acquired it for me with Your precious blood, in homage to Your divine justice, to bring about the fulfilment of Your designs in my regard, so that I may love and glorify You ever more perfectly.

Confidence and Self-Abandonment in the Hands of God

Humility is the mother of confidence. When you realize that you are destitute of all good and of every virtue, and of all power and capacity to serve God, and that you are a true hell full of all kinds of evil, you can no longer rely in any way upon yourself, or upon what is yours. You are obliged to emerge from yourself, as you would go out of hell, to enter into Jesus as into Paradise, where you find in great abundance all that is lacking in yourself. You must place your reliance and trust in Him, as in the One given to you by your eternal Father to be your redemption, your justice, your virtue, your sanctification, your treasure, your strength, your life and your all. It is to this that He would draw you when He lovingly and compellingly urges you to come to Him with confidence, saying:

> *"Come to Me, all you who labor, and are burdened, and I will refresh you"* (Matt. 11:28),

and will relieve you of the weight of your sorrows. Our Lord assures us that He will reject no one who will come to Him:

> *"All that the Father gives to Me shall come to Me; and he that comes to Me, I will not cast out"* (John 6:37).

In order to compel us to become confident, He tells us in various texts of holy Scripture that

> accursed and wretched are they who place their trust in any other thing but Him; but happy and blessed are they who entrust themselves to Him (Jer. 17:5-7);

> they shall abound in all kinds of graces and blessings, and shall lack nothing (Ps. 23).

> His eyes are fixed upon those who hope in His mercy (Ps. 33:18).

> He is good to those who, hope in Him (Lam. 3:25).

> His mercy shall compass them about (Ps. 31:10)

81

He Himself will always be by their side (Prov. 3:26).

He is the shield of all that trust in Him (II Samuel 22:31 – NRSV-CE; II Kings, 22:31 – Douay);

He is their protector and helper (Ps. 113:5-9).

He will protect them in His tabernacle and He will hide them in the secret of His face (Ps. 31:20),

or, as another version has it,

"as the apple of his eye" (Ps. 17:8).

He will be their defense in the day of trial, and will help them and deliver them from the hands of sinners because they have put their trust in Him (Ps. 91:14-15);

He will let them taste in its perfection the great multitude of His sweetness (Ps. 31:19);

they will always be full of joy, and He will abide in them (Ps. 5:11-12).

He lavishes upon them His graces and the effects of His mercy, in proportion to the hope and confidence they have in Him (Ps. 33:22);

those who trust in Him will know truth (Wis. 3:9),

that is He the sovereign truth will manifest Himself to those who trust in Him; they will not sin,

or, according to the Hebrew version,

they will not be condemned and will not perish,

that is,

He will not allow them to fall into sins that would separate them from Him and reduce them to perdition (Ps. 34:22);

those who place their hope in Him will sanctify themselves as He is sanctified (I John 3:3).

Never has anyone who entrusted himself to Him been disappointed or defrauded of his expectations (Sirach 2:10 – NRSV-CE; Eccli. 2:11 – Douay).

God grants to them everything that they confidently ask of Him (Matt. 21:22).

Finally,

nothing is impossible to those who have faith and confidence in Him, but they can accomplish all things, relying on His goodness and power (Mark 9:22-23).

I could go on forever, if I began to quote here all the texts from holy Scripture in which God commends to you the virtue of trust. It seems as if He were not satisfied even with the thousand instances in holy Scripture by which He proves how dear and delightful this holy virtue is to Him, and how much He loves and favors those who place their trust in His goodness and abandon themselves entirely to the fatherly care of His divine providence.

You may read in the third book of *Intimations of Divine Piety* [*Herald of Divine Love*], by St. Gertrude, that Jesus once told her that the filial confidence of a Christian soul is the eye of the holy spouse, of which the divine Bridegroom says in the Canticle of Canticles [Song of Songs]:

"You have wounded my heart, my sister, my spouse: you have wounded my heart by one of your eyes" (Song 4:9).

In other words, the soul that has firm confidence in Christ, and trusts that He can, and desires, to help it faithfully in all things, pierces His heart right through with an arrow of love; and such confidence does such violence to the piety of Jesus that He can in no way absent Himself from it.

St. Mechtilde's [Matilda] *Book of Special Grace* [*Love of the Sacred Heart*] tells us that Jesus said to her also:

"It is a special delight to Me when men trust in My goodness and rely upon Me. And so, whoever shall have great trust in Me, yet always with humility, shall be favored by Me in this life, and in the next receive more than he deserves. The more anyone trusts in Me and avails himself of My goodness, the greater will be his gain, since it is impossible for a man not to obtain what he believes with holy conviction, and hopes to gain because it has been promised him. And so it is most advantageous to a man to have firm trust in Me, when he hopes for great things from Me!"

Again, when St. Mechtilde asked God what the main thing was that she should believe of His ineffable goodness, He replied:

"Firmly believe that after death I will receive you as a father receives a dear son, and that no father ever so faithfully and lovingly gave all his possessions to an only son, as I will make you a sharer in all that is Mine. Whoever shall believe this of My goodness, firmly and with humble charity, will be happy indeed."

Additional Points on Confidence

To strengthen you further in holy confidence, our most gentle and amiable Savior gives Himself all the most sweet and loving names and qualities imaginable, to describe His relationship with you. He calls Himself:

- your friend,
- your advocate,
- your physician,
- your shepherd,
- your brother,
- your father,
- your soul,
- your spirit
- and the Bridegroom of your soul.

He calls you:

- His sheep,
- His brethren,
- His children,
- His portion,
- His heritage,
- His soul,
- His heart.

Your soul he regards as His cherished spouse. At various places in Sacred Scripture. He assures you that

He exercises continual care and watchfulness over you (I Peter 5:7);

He carries you, and will always carry you in His heart and in His bosom (Isa. 46:3-4).

Nor is He satisfied with saying once or twice that He bears you so tenderly. He repeats this beautiful thought as many as five times in a single passage.

Elsewhere He says that

even if a mother were to forget the child she bore in her womb, He would never forget you, and that He has written you in His hands, that He might always have you before His eyes (Isa. 49:15-17);

whoever touches you touches the apple of His eye (Zach. 2:8);

you should have no care for the things that are necessary to you to sustain life and clothe yourself; He well knows that you need such things, and He takes care of them on your behalf (Matt. 6:31-33);

He has numbered every hair of your head (Matt. 10:30),

and of these, not one shall perish (Luke 21:18):

His Father loves you as He loves the Son Himself and the Son loves you as He is loved by His Father (John 15:9);

He wants you to be where He is, that is, to be at rest with Him in the bosom and heart of His Father (John 17:24),

to sit with Him upon His throne (Rev. 3:21),

In a word, He wants you to be one with Him, and, indeed, to be consummated in unity with Him and with the Father of heaven (John 17:21-23).

If you have offended Him, He promises, provided you come back to Him with humility, repentance, confidence in His goodness, and the resolution to make a clean break with sin, that He will receive you, He will embrace you, He will forget all your sins, and clothe you with the garment of His grace and His love, of which you had been stripped by your sins (Ezech. 18:21; Luke 15:22).

Who, after all this, will not have confidence? Who will not become entirely abandoned to the care and guidance of a Brother, a Father, a Bridegroom, endowed with infinite wisdom to know what is most advantageous for you and to foresee everything that could possibly happen to you, and to select the most appropriate means to bring you to the goal of your supreme happiness? Not only this, but He is also filled with extreme goodness with which He wills all kinds of good for you, together with immense power to turn aside any evil which might befall you, and to pour forth upon you the complete wealth of benefits He wills to grant you.

Lest you think His words and promises ineffectual, look for a moment at all He did and suffered for you in His Incarnation, His life, His Passion, and His death, as well as the wonderful graces He still brings to us daily in the blessed sacrament of the Eucharist. Consider how He came down from heaven to earth, out of love for you, how He humbled Himself to the extent of willing to become a little child, to be born in a stable and embrace all the woes and needs of a human and mortal life. See how He devoted all His hours, all His thoughts, words, and actions to you; how He delivered up His holy body to Pilate, to the executioners and to the cross; how He laid down His life and shed His blood even to the last drop; how He gives you every day, in the holy Eucharist, His body, His blood, His soul, His divinity, all His riches, all that He is, all that is most dear and most precious to Him.

> O You who are goodness! O Love! O most great and amiable Jesus! Let them trust in You, who know Your Name (Ps. 9:10), which is none other than love and goodness, for You are all love, all goodness and all mercy. Yet I am not surprised that there should be so few who trust in You perfectly, since there are so few who study themselves to find out and observe the effects of Your infinite goodness. O my Savior, surely I am most worthless if I do not have confidence in Your goodness, after You have displayed so very many proofs of Your love for me! If You have done and suffered so much, and if You have given us such great things, what would You not do yet again, what would You not add now to, these gifts, if only I came to You with humility and confidence?

Cultivate a great desire to be firmly rooted in the sublime virtue of confidence. Do not fear but be courageous in serving and loving our most adorable and amiable Jesus, with great perfection and holiness. Undertake courageously great tasks for His glory, in proportion to the power and grace He will give you for this end. Even though you can do nothing of yourself, you can do all things in Him and His help will never fail you, if you have confidence in His goodness.

Place your entire physical and spiritual welfare in His hands. Abandon to the paternal solicitude of His divine providence every care for your health, reputation, property and business, for those near to you, for your past sins, for your soul's progress in virtue and love of Him, for your life, death and especially for your salvation and eternity, in a word, all your cares. Rest in the assurance that, in His pure goodness, He will watch with particular tenderness over all your responsibilities and cares and dispose all things for the greatest good.

Do not rely on the power or influence of friends, on your own money, on your intellect, knowledge or strength, on your good desires and resolutions, or on human means, or on any created thing, but on God's mercy alone. You may, of course, use all these things and take advantage of every aid that you can marshal on your side to conquer vice, to practice virtue, to direct and conclude all the business that God has placed in your hands, and acquit yourself of the obligations of your state in life. Certainly, you must renounce all dependence or confidence you may have in these things, to rely upon Our Lord's goodness alone. You ought to take as much pain and work as hard for your own part, as if you expected nothing from God: nevertheless, you should no more rely upon your own resources and labor than if you had done nothing at all but had looked to God's mercy alone for all things.

To this we are exhorted by the Holy Spirit, saying, by the mouth of David, the royal prophet:

> *"Commit your way to the Lord, and trust in Him, and He will do it"* (Ps. 37:5).

And in another place:

> *"Cast your care upon the Lord and he shall sustain you"* (Ps. 55:22).

Also, speaking through St. Peter, the Prince of the Apostles, He advises us to

> cast all our cares and worries upon God, since He watches over us (I Peter 5:7).

This is what Our Lord said to St. Catherine of Sienna:

> "Daughter, forget yourself and think of Me, and I will ever think of you."

Accept this teaching as if addressed to you personally and to no one else. Let your chief care be to avoid everything that displeases Our Lord, trying to serve and love Him perfectly, and He will turn everything, even your faults, to your advantage.

Acquire the habit of making frequent Acts of Trust in God, but especially when you happen to be assailed by thoughts or feelings of fear and mistrust, either with regard to your past sins, or for any other reason. At such times lift up your heart at once to Jesus, and say to Him, with the royal prophet:

> *"To You, O Lord, have I lifted up my soul. In You, O my God, I put my trust; let me not be ashamed"* (Ps. 24:1-2).

> *"In You, O Lord, have I hoped, let me never be confounded"* (Ps. 31:1).

> *"My God, in him will I trust"* (Ps. 90:2).

> *"The Lord is my helper: I will not fear what man can do unto me"* (Ps. 118:6).

> *"The Lord is my helper and I will look over my enemies"* (Ps. 118:7).

"It is good to confide in the Lord, rather than to have confidence in man" (Ps. 118:8).

"For though I should walk in the midst of the shadow of death, I will fear no evils, for You are with me" (Ps. 23:4).

Or else join the prophet Isaias, saying:

"Behold, God is my Savior, I will deal confidently and will not fear" (Isa. 12:2).

Or say with holy Job:

"Although He should kill me, I will trust in Him" (Job 13:15).

Or, repeat the words of the poor man in the Gospel:

"I do believe, Lord: help my unbelief " (Mark 9:23).

At other times, say with the holy apostles:

"Lord, increase our faith" (Luke 17:5).

Or else speak to Him thus:

"O good Jesus, it is in You alone that I have placed all my trust. O You My strength and only refuge, I give and abandon myself entirely to You; do with me whatever You please."

"Oh my sweet love, O my dear hope, I place my whole being in Your hands and sacrifice it to You, with my life, my soul and all that belongs to me, that You may dispose of them in time and in eternity howsoever it pleases You, for Your glory!"

In conclusion, confidence is a gift of God that follows in the wake of humility and love. Therefore, ask it of God, and He will give it to you. Strive to perform your every action in a spirit of humility for the pure love of God, and you will soon taste the sweetness and peace that accompany the virtue of confidence.

ADDENDA

A Note on the Translator

In late 1941, the young **Thomas Merton** left his existence in the world to seek the freedom of cloistered life.

At the Trappist Abbey of Our Lady of Gethsemani novices were immersed in work and silence for two years before beginning serious study. Because of his mastery of language, one assignment given to the young frater (as novices were then called) was to translate certain spiritual classics from French. During Lent of 1943, he was given *The Life and Kingdom of Jesus* by St. John Eudes with an aggressive deadline for completion. His early autobiography describes the harrowing work:

> "After the Conventual Mass, I would get out book and pencil and papers and go to work at one of the long tables in the novitiate scriptorium, filling the yellow sheets as fast as I could, while another novice took them and typed them as soon as they were finished."[1]

Despite this pressure from the publisher, the project was completed on time. Merton's superior called the finished product "the best translation of any of the works of St. John Eudes that he had seen."[2] Archbishop Fulton Sheen agreed in his introduction to this edition of *The Kingdom*, exulting that the spiritual treatise was "now so ably translated into English."[3]

This took place years before Merton's "Seven Storey Mountain" was released to the public, so his name did not yet hold great value to the publishers. In the spirit of humility and silence, Merton accepted for his translation to be attributed simply to "A Trappist Father in The Abbey of Our Lady of Gethsemani."[4]

1   Thomas Merton, *The Seven Storey Mountain* (New York: Harcourt, Brace & Company, 1948), 401.

2   Benjamin Clark, OCSO, "Thomas Merton's Gethsemani: Part 1, the Novitiate Years," *The Merton Annual, vol. 4* (1991): 250.

3   Fulton J Sheen, Introduction to *The Life and Kingdom of Jesus in Christian Souls*, by St. John Eudes (New York: PJ Kennedy & Sons, 1946), xix.

4   The attribution to a "Trappist *father*" is curious given that Merton would not be ordained until 1949. However, there is no doubt that the work is his. Fr. Benjamin Clark OCSO was the "other novice" referred to in the Seven Storey Mountain. Fr. Clark recalls:

"I remember one such assignment which Merton records (SSM, p. 401). Gethsemani had entered a contract to translate the work of St. John Eudes for the publication of a new edition. Several of the monks had been assigned volumes to translate, and Merton was given The Kingdom of Jesus in Christian Souls. The publishers had allowed only a short time for the work to be completed and so I was assigned to help Merton meet the deadline. I typed the finished copy in triplicate as Merton dashed off the original on sheets of yellow paper." "Thomas Merton's Gethsemani," p. 249.

About St. John Eudes

Born in France on November 14, 1601, St. John Eudes' life spanned the "Great Century." The Age of Discovery had revolutionized technology and exploration; the Council of Trent initiated a much-needed reform in the Church; among the common people, it was the dawn of a golden age of sanctity and mystic fervor.

His Spiritual Heritage

No fewer than seven Doctors of the Church had lived in the previous century. Great reformers like St. Francis de Sales, St. Teresa of Avila, and St. John of the Cross had left an indelible mark on the Catholic faith. Their influence was still fresh as St. John Eudes came onto the scene.

He was educated by the Jesuits in rural Normandy. He was ordained into the Oratory of Jesus and Mary, a society of priests which had just been founded on the model of St. Philip Neri's Oratory in Rome. The founder was Cardinal Pierre de Bérulle, a man renowned for his holiness and named "the apostle of the Incarnate Word" by Pope Urban VII. Rounding out St. John Eudes' heritage is the influence of the Discalced Carmelites. His spiritual director, Cardinal Bérulle himself, had brought sisters from St. Teresa of Avila's convent to help found the Carmel in France. John Eudes would later become spiritual director to a Carmelite convent himself. Their cloister prayed constantly for his missionary activity.

His Life of Ministry

As an avid participant in a wave of re-evangelization in France, St. John Eudes' principal apostolate was preaching parish missions. Spending anywhere from 4 to 20 weeks in each parish, he preached over 120 missions across his lifetime, always with a team of confessors providing the sacrament around the clock, and catechists meeting daily with small groups of parishioners.

Early in his priesthood, an outbreak of plague hit St. John Eudes' native region and he rushed to provide sacraments to the dying. The risk of contagion was so great no one else dared to approach the victims. In order to protect his Oratorian brothers from contagion, St. John Eudes took up residence in a large empty cider barrel outside of the city walls until the plague had ended.

His Foundations

During his missions he heard countless confessions himself, including those from women forced into prostitution. Realizing that they needed intense healing and support, he began to found "Houses of Refuge" to help them get off the street and begin a new life. In 1641 he founded the Sisters of Our Lady of Charity of the Refuge to continue this work. They would live with the penitent women and provide them with constant support. Today, these sisters are known as the Good Shepherd Sisters, inspired by their fourth vow of zeal to go out seeking the "lost sheep."

Occasionally, St. John Eudes would return to the site of a previous mission. To his dismay, he found that the fruits of the mission were consistently fading for lack of support. The crucial piece in need of change was the priesthood. At that time, the only way to be trained as a priest was through apprenticeship. The result of this training was so horribly inconsistent that the term "hocus pocus" was invented during this time to describe the corrupted Latin used by poorly trained priests during the consecration at mass. In 1643 he left the Oratory and founded the Congregation of Jesus and Mary to found a seminary. Seminary training was a radical brand-new concept which had just been proposed by the Council of Trent.

His Mark on the Church

At a mission in 1648 St. John Eudes authored the first mass in history in honor of the Heart of Mary. In 1652 he built the first church under the Immaculate Heart's patronage: the chapel of his seminary in Coutances, France. During the process of his canonization, Pope St. Pius X named St. John Eudes "the father, doctor, and apostle of liturgical devotion to the hearts of Jesus and Mary." The Heart of Jesus because he created the first Feast of the Sacred Heart in 1672, just one year before St. Margaret Mary Alacoque had her first apparition of the Sacred Heart.

Although his Marian devotion was intense from a tender age, the primary inspiration for this feast came from St. John Eudes' theology of baptism. From the beginning of his missionary career he taught that Jesus continues His Incarnation in the life of each baptized Christian. As we give ourselves to Christ, our hands become His hands, our heart is transformed into His heart. Mary is the ultimate exemplar of this. She gave her heart to God so completely that she and Jesus have just one heart between them. Thus, whoever sees Mary, sees Jesus, and honoring the heart of Mary is never separate from honoring the heart of Jesus.

le Blond pinxt   P. Drevet Sculpsit

Le Venerable Jean Eudes Instituteur de la Congregation de Jesus et Marie
de l'Ordre de Notre-Dame de Charité et de la Societé du S. Cœur de la mere Admirable

Doctor of the Church?

At the time of this writing, Bishops the world over have requested that the Vatican proclaim St. John Eudes as a Doctor of the Church. This would recognize his unique contribution to our understanding of the Gospel, and his exemplary holiness of life which stands out even among saints. For more information on the progress of this cause, on his writings or spirituality, or to sign up for our e-newsletter updates, contact spirituality@eudistsusa.org.

About the Eudist Family

During his lifetime, St. John Eudes' missionary activity had three major areas of focus.

- For priests, he provided formation, education, and the spiritual support which is crucial for their role in God's plan of salvation.
- For prostitutes and others on the margins of society, he gave them a home and bound their wounds, like the Good Shepherd with his lost sheep.
- For the laity, he preached the dignity of their baptism and their responsibility to be the hands and feet of God, to continue the Incarnation.

In everything he did, he burned with the desire to be a living example of the love and mercy of God.

These are the "family values" which continue to inspire those who continue his work. To paraphrase St. Paul, John Eudes planted seeds, which others watered through the institutions he founded, and God gave the growth. Today, the family tree continues to bear fruit:

The *Congregation of Jesus and Mary* (CJM), also known as The Eudists, continues the effort to form and care for priests and other leaders within the Church. St. John Eudes called this the mission of "teaching the teachers, shepherding the shepherds, and enlightening those who are the light of the world." Continuing his efforts as a missionary preacher, Eudist priests and brothers "audaciously seek to open up new avenues for evangelization," through television, radio, and new media.

The *Religious of the Good Shepherd* (RGS) continue outreach to women in difficult situations, providing them with a deeply needed place of refuge and healing while they seek a new life. St. Mary Euphrasia drastically expanded the reach of this mission which now operates in over 70 countries worldwide. A true heiress of St. John Eudes, St. Mary Euphrasia exhorted her sisters: "We must go after the lost sheep with no other rest than the cross, no other consolation than work, and no other thirst than for justice."

In every seminary and House of Refuge founded by St. John Eudes, he also established a *Confraternity of the Holy Heart of Jesus and Mary* for the laity, now known as the Eudist Associates. The mission he gave them was twofold: First, "To glorify the divine Hearts of Jesus and Mary... working to make them live and reign in their own heart through diligent imitation of their virtues." Second, "To work for the salvation of souls... by practicing, according to their abilities, works of charity and mercy and by attaining numerous graces through prayer for the clergy and other apostolic laborers."

The *Little Sisters of the Poor* were an outgrowth of this confraternity. St. Jeanne Jugan was formed as a consecrated woman within the Eudist Family. She discovered the great need for love and mercy among the poor and elderly and the mission took on a life of its own. She passed on to them the Eudist intuition that the poor are not simply recipients of charity, they provide an encounter with Charity Himself: "My little ones, never forget that the poor are Our Lord... In serving the aged, it is He Himself whom you are serving."

A more recent "sprout" on the tree was founded by Mother Antonia Brenner in Tijuana, Mexico. After raising her children in Beverly Hills and suffering through divorce, she followed God's call to become a live-in prison minister at the *La Mesa* penitentiary. The *Eudist Servants of the 11th Hour* was founded so that other women in the latter part of their lives could imitate her in "being love" to those most in need.

The example St. John Eudes set for living out the Gospel has inspired many more individuals and organizations throughout the world. For more information about the Eudist family, news on upcoming publications, or for ways to share in our mission, contact us at spirituality@eudistsusa.org.

On the Threshold of Eternity: A Self-Directed Retreat to Prepare for a Happy Death

For more from St. John Eudes, Eudist Press offers individual prayerbooks that shine a spotlight on different aspects of his spirituality. Each one is an excerpt from his classic bestseller: *The Life and the Kingdom of Jesus: A Treatise on Christian Perfection for Use by Clergy or Laity,* translated from French by Thomas Merton in The Abbey of Our Lady of Gethsémani and published by Kennedy & Sons in New York, 1946.

They can be found at https://www.eudistsusa.org/publications.

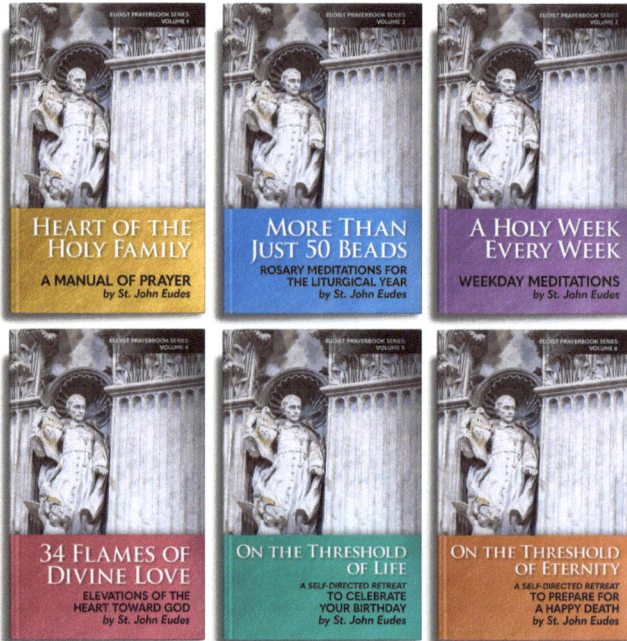

More by Eudist Press
- *A Heart on Fire: St. John Eudes, a Model for the New Evangelization*
- *Spiritual Itinerary for Today with St. John Eudes*
- *Eudist Lectionary: A St. John Eudes Reader*

Eudist Prayerbook Series
- Volume 1: *Heart of the Holy Family:*
  A Manual of Prayer
- Volume 2: *More than Just 50 Beads:*
  Rosary Meditations for the Liturgical Year
- Volume 3: *A Holy Week Every Week:*
  Weekday Meditations
- Volume 4: *34 Flames of Divine Love:*
  Elevations of the Heart Towards God
- Volume 5: *On the Threshold of Life:*
  A Self-Directed Retreat to Celebrate your Birthday
- Volume 6: *On the Threshold of Eternity:*
  A Self-Directed Retreat to Prepare for a Happy Death

Biography
- *St. John Eudes: An Artisan of Christian Renewal of the Seventeenth Century*
- *In All Things, the Will of God: St. John Eudes Through His Letters*

More by St. John Eudes
St. John Eudes' Selected Works
- *The Life and Kingdom of Jesus in Christian Souls*
- *The Sacred Heart of Jesus*
- *The Admirable Heart of Mary*
- *The Priest: His Dignity and Obligations*
- *Meditations*
- *Letters and Shorter Works*

Other Works
- *Man's Contract with God in Holy Baptism*
- *The Wondrous Childhood of the Mother of God*

EUDIST PRESS

www.ingramcontent.com/pod-product-compliance
Lightning Source LLC
Chambersburg PA
CBHW042128080426
42735CB00001B/2